As SAINTS WE SING

As SAINTS WE SING

MICHAEL D. YOUNG

CFI
An imprint of Cedar Fort, Inc.
Springville, Utah

ISBN 13: 978-1-4621-4028-2

Published by CFI, an imprint of Cedar Fort, Inc.
2373 W. 700 S., Springville, UT 84663
Distributed by Cedar Fort, Inc., www.cedarfort.com

Library of Congress Control Number: 2021939450

Cover design by Courtney Proby

Edited by Luci Jones

Printed in the United States of America

10 9 8 7 6 5 4 3 2 1

Printed on acid-free paper

Dedication

To all those who serve
God through music

Acknowledgments

Putting together this hymnbook is not something that could have been done alone. I want to acknowledge the many wonderful people who gave of their time and talents to make this collection a reality.

I want to thank Glenn Gordon for helping me solidify so many things about this hymnbook and for providing much needed motivation.

I want to thank those who served on the selection committee, including Jason Robison, Glenn Gordon, Luke Howard, Glenn Nelson, Michael Collings, Joan Sowards, Brady Allred, Eda Ashby, Jay Ruben Williams, Kathy Blanco, Andy Schow, Donna Howard, Kurt Kammeyer, Nathan Howe, and Garrett Breeze.

In addition, Nathan Howe created the template for the hymns and provided much needed support.

I would like to acknowledge the composers and lyricists who contributed to this collection. An alphabetical list of their names is included on page xviii of this volume.

Finally, a special thanks goes to those who helped edit the collection, including Jana McGettigan, Amber Gurr, Douglas Allan, Esther Megargel, Kathleen Holyoak, Nachelle Sampson, Sarah Coley, Doug Flory, Catherine Cheney, Charity Davis, Shaillé Claypool, Klinton Helms, and Nathan Howe.

Preface

The idea of putting together this collection came several years ago after visiting a sacrament meeting with a friend and hearing a ward choir give a special musical number. The number was heartfelt, but while I was listening to it, I had a thought come into my mind: how much better could ward choirs be if they had more resources and training?

So many people I have talked to over the years have found themselves suddenly holding a ward music calling without really knowing what direction to take it. Of course, church music does not have to be technically perfect in order to be effective, but if my years singing with the Mormon Tabernacle Choir have taught me anything, it is that the Lord magnifies our efforts when we give all that we can give and do all that we can do. The directors of the choir, Mack Wilberg and Ryan Murphy, have always been relentless in their pursuit of excellence and even the elusive prize of perfection. We are commanded to improve ourselves in other areas of our lives, so why should music be any different?

In response to these thoughts, I embarked on a two-pronged project. The first part was a book called *The Song of the Righteous*, which talks about the ins and outs of ward choir, for both those who run ward choirs and those who sing in ward choirs. It was published by Covenant Communications in October 2017.

The second is this collection, which has been several years in the making. I have been completely overwhelmed with the outpouring of support I have experienced from other Latter-day Saint musicians and authors.

With a collection like this, I would certainly be remiss if I did not mention the guidance and inspiration of our Heavenly Father. He is the author of all good things, and this collection represents an offering of the time, talents, and resources of many as a way to thank and serve Him.

—Michael D. Young, 2018

About This Collection

This hymnbook is separated into several sections, and the hymns in each section are arranged alphabetically. The sections are as follows:

General Hymns: These are hymns written by Latter-day Saint composers and lyricists that do not fall into a special category. They are all original works, and many of them are appearing for the first time in this collection.

Sacrament Hymns: These are hymns that focus on the atoning work of Jesus Christ and would be especially appropriate for a sacrament meeting.

New Settings: These are existing hymns—many of which are from the Latter-day Saint tradition—that are set to new music.

Christmas Hymns: These hymns—some of which are original to this collection—are especially appropriate for the Christmas season.

New Christmas Settings: These Christmas hymns are existing hymns set to new music.

Easter Hymns: These hymns—some of which are original to this collection—are especially appropriate for the Easter season.

Priesthood/Relief Society Hymns: These hymns are set for only men's voices or only women's voices.

Benedictions: These hymns are appropriate for concluding meetings.

The hymns in this collection are not meant to replace the regular Latter-day Saint hymnal but are intended to supplement worship with doctrinally appropriate songs.

We would enjoy hearing from those who have used this collection. If you have any questions, comments, or suggestions, please contact Michael Young at thesongoftherighteous@gmail.com.

Contents

By Section

General Hymns

1 Act Well Thy Part
2 A Great and Marv'lous Work Is Ours
3 Abide the Day
4 All Creation Doth Reverence Thy Majesty, Lord
5 All Things Denote
6 All Things Renew
7 Arise O Glorious Zion
8 As God Has Given Life to Me
9 As Thou Hast Fed the Multitude
10 Awake, My Soul
11 Be Ye Therefore Perfect
12 Beauty for Ashes
13 Beside Still Waters
14 Blessed Are the Pure in Heart
15 Blessed, Arise, Your Time Has Come
16 By Faith
17 By Lives of Charity
18 Can Ye Feel So Now?
19 Choose You This Day
20 Christ the Lord Is Ever Near
21 Come Join the Ranks of Zion's Grand Army
22 Come to the Mountain of the Lord
23 Come to the Temple
24 Crown after Cross
25 Endurance
26 Enduring to the End

27	Enjoy the Journey
28	Every Hymn I Bear toward Zion
29	Father, Hear Us Lift One Voice
30	Fullness Restored
31	God Looks upon the Heart
32	Have Thine Own Way, Lord
33	Hearken to the Prophets
34	He Is My Cornerstone
35	Help Is Wanted
36	Holy Temples
37	How Great Is Our Lord
38	How Sweet the Spirit's Beckoning
39	How Sweet to Me!
40	I'll Follow Jesus Christ
41	In the Savior's Name
42	I Will Follow Christ
43	I Worship God
44	Jesus Is My Savior
45	Let Me, Oh Lord, Lead Others to Thee
46	Let Us Bow before His Throne
47	Lord, Accept Our Offering
48	Lord, May I Not Forget
49	Love Is a Daily Choice
50	May Thy Daystar Rise in Me
51	Memorial Day
52	Moroni's Golden Trumpet
53	My Joy Is in Thy Service, Lord
54	My Life Is But a Weaving
55	No Matter What I May Achieve
56	No Purer Love
57	Now Is the Hour for Faith, Not Fear
58	Oh Jesus, Savior of Mankind

59 Oh, to Have Been in Kirtland
60 Our Birth Is But a Sleep
61 Prayer of Thanks
62 Raise Your Voices to the Lord
63 Rejoice as Saints of the Latter Days
64 Rejoice, Rejoice, Rejoice
65 Restoration Morning
66 Share Goodness
67 Sing All Praise to God the Father
68 Stick of Joseph, Stick of Judah
69 Thanksgiving
70 The Book of Mormon
71 The Disciple's Prayer
72 The Father, Son, and Holy Ghost
73 The Gospel of Our Lord
74 The One Sure Light
75 The Promised Day Must Soon Break Forth
76 There Is No Place So Far Away
77 The Restoration
78 The Sabbath Is a Sweet Delight
79 The Song of Redeeming Love
80 Thunder Must Roar
81 Two Birds That Sing from Branches High
82 Upon Wings of Prayer
83 We Add Our Voice
84 What Greater Peace?
85 When Godly Sorrow Moves the Soul
86 When the Savior Comes Again

Sacrament Hymns

87 Always Remember Him
88 As If from Thine Own Wounded Hand

89	Bread of Life and Living Water
90	Heal Our Souls
91	His Love Divine
92	I Did, Too
93	In Gethsemane
94	In Token of Christ's Sacrifice
95	O Savior Dear
96	Our Savior
97	Our Savior in Gethsemane
98	Redeemed and Renewed
99	Repentance
100	Sacrament
101	The Last Supper
102	White As Wool and Clean Again

New Settings

103	A Poor Wayfaring Man of Grief
104	Behold the Great Redeemer Die
105	Christ the Lord Is Risen Today
106	Come, Follow Me
107	Come Unto Jesus
108	Dearest Children, God Is Near You
109	For the Beauty of the Earth
110	Hark, All Ye Nations
111	Have I Done Any Good?
112	How Gentle God's Commands
113	I Need Thee Every Hour
114	I Saw a Mighty Angel Fly
115	I Stand All Amazed
116	I'll Go Where You Want Me to Go
117	I'm a Pilgrim, I'm a Stranger
118	In Hymns of Praise

119	Jesus, the Very Thought of Thee
120	Joseph Smith's First Prayer
121	Let Us All Press On
122	Nearer, My God, to Thee
123	O My Father
124	Praise to the Man
125	Precious Savior, Dear Redeemer
126	Put Your Shoulder to the Wheel
127	Reverently and Meekly Now
128	Sweet Is the Work
129	The Spirit of God
130	When through the Deep Waters
131	Ye Elders of Israel

Christmas Hymns

132	A Cradle Hymn
133	A Day without Night
134	Blessed Baby, Savior of Men
135	Christmas Star
136	Glory Hallelujah!
137	Holy Was That Wondrous Night
138	How Precious the Hope
139	I Am the Light
140	In Bethlehem There Lies a King
141	In David's Lowly City
142	Let the Earth and Angels Sing
143	Little Lamb
144	My Heart Will Always Linger
145	Sing Hallelujah!
146	The City of David
147	The Night Was Still

New Christmas Settings

148 Away in a Manger
149 I Heard the Bells on Christmas Day
150 It Came upon the Midnight Clear
151 O Come, All Ye Faithful
152 O Holy Night
153 Silent Night
154 With Wondering Awe

Easter Hymns

155 Early That Morn
156 He Walked Alone so We Must Not
157 On Easter Morn
158 Resurrection Hymn

Relief Society and Priesthood

159 Bearers of God's Holy Priesthood
160 Charity, Never Failing
161 Daughters in His Kingdom
162 God's Infinite, Eternal Power
163 I Am Naught without My Savior
164 Live Up to Your Privilege
165 Priesthood Blessings
166 Priesthood Power
167 Steadfast and Immovable
168 The Priesthood Is Restored
169 The Priesthood Keys

Benedictions

170 A Part of You
171 God, Be Thou with Me
172 God Be with You Till We Meet Again

173	God Welcomes His Servants Back Home
174	Old Irish Blessing
175	The Lord Bless You and Keep You
176	When Shall We All Meet Again?

List of Contributors

Abplanalp, Hillary	Composer/Lyricist
Adams, Sarah F.	Lyricist
Addison, Joseph	Composer/Lyricist
Allan, Douglas W.	Composer/Lyricist
Alexander, Cecil F.	Lyricist
Anderson, Charles V.	Lyricist
Ashdown, Donald	Lyricist
Ashdown, Franklin D.	Composer
Atkins, George	Lyricist
Auerbach, Herbert	Lyricist
Babcock, Malthie D.	Lyricist
Bach, Johann S.	Composer
Bain, J. L. Macbeth	Lyricist
Baker, Henry W.	Lyricist
Baker, Theodore	Lyricist
Baring-Gould, Sabine	Lyricist
Barthelemon, Francois H.	Composer
Beesley, Ebeneezer	Lyricist
Beethoven, Ludwig Van	Composer
Belliston, Rebecca	Composer
Benson, Louis F.	Lyricist
Bernotski, Jared	Composer
Blenkhorn, Ada	Lyricist
Bliss, Phillip P.	Composer
Boyd, Norma	Composer/Lyricist

Borthwick, Jane L.	Lyricist
Bradbury, William B.	Composer
Bridges, Matthew	Lyricist
Brown, Mary	Lyricist
Burkett, J. C.	Lyricist
Burnett, Nora Kay	Composer
Bryne, Mary E.	Lyricist
Campbell, Joan D.	Lyricist
Campbell, Hal K.	Composer
Card, Orson Scott	Lyricist
Carter, Russel Kelso	Composer/Lyricist
Caswall, Edward	Composer
Clairvaux, Bernard of	Lyricist
Claypool, Shaillé Elder	Composer/Lyricist
Cole, Benjamin	Composer
Coles, George	Composer
Cornelius, Maxwell N.	Lyricist
Croxall, Gary	Lyricist
Dickman, Annette W.	Composer/Lyricist
Draper, Christian S.	Composer/Lyricist
Doldridge, Phillip	Lyricist
Dwight, John Sullivan	Lyricist
Faure, Gabriel	Composer
Featherstone, David	Composer/Lyricist
Fletcher, Phineas	Lyricist
Frost, Laurel	Lyricist
Fotheringham, Mark R.	Lyricist
Gabriel, Charles H.	Lyricist
Gates, Peter	Composer/Lyricist
Gauntlet, Henry J.	Composer
Gibbons, Orlando	Composer
Gilbert, Susan	Lyricist
Graham, Rick	Composer/Lyricist
Glenn, Sharlee	Lyricist
Gruber, Franz	Lyricist
Hadlock, Lyle	Composer/Lyricist
Hampton, Bradley	Composer/Lyricist
Hawks, Anne S.	Lyricist

Havergal, Frances R.	Lyricist
Hegy, Grace	Composer/Lyricist
Herbert, George	Lyricist
Holden, Oliver	Composer
Holmes, Oliver Wendell Sr.	Lyricist
Holst, Gustav	Composer
Holyoak, Kathleen	Composer
Howe, Nathan	Composer/Lyricist
Hudson, Ralph E.	Composer
Huish, Orson Pratt	Lyricist
Hunzinger, Linda	Lyricist
Jensen, Kim	Lyricist
Keen, Marta	Composer
Keen, Robert	Lyricist
Kerr, Daniel	Composer
Killburn, Dianne	Lyricist
Killian, Angie Mae	Lyricist
Kilmer, Joyce	Lyricist
Knapp, Phoebe P.	Composer
Kocherhans, Jeff	Composer/Lyricist
Larsen, Ryan	Composer/Lyricist
Leavitt, John C.	Composer
Longfellow, William W.	Lyricist
Longstaff, William D.	Lyricist
Lowry, Robert	Lyricist
Luther, Martin	Lyricist
Macfarlane, David	Lyricist
Malan, Henri A. C.	Composer
Malizia, Eric	Lyricist
Mann, Charles	Composer
Manwaring, George	Lyricist
Mason, Lowell	Composer
Matheson, George	Lyricist
McGettigan, Jana	Composer
McGranahan, James	Composer
McKee, Dianne Williams	Composer/Lyricist
McNeely, Kimberly N.	Composer
McNeely, Randall D.	Lyricist
Mead, Hyrum	Lyricist

Mead, Rosemary	Composer
Megargel, Esther	Composer
Mendelssohn, Felix	Composer
Mercer, Daniel R.	Lyricist
Merill, William P.	Lyricist
Miess, Stephanie	Composer/Lyricist
Milan, Ambrose of	Lyricist
Miles, C. Austin	Composer/Lyricist
Millis, William G.	Lyricist
Minor, George	Composer
Moench, Louis F.	Lyricist
Montez, Dan	Composer
Montgomery, James	Lyricist
Moore, Andrew	Composer/Lyricist
Moore, William	Composer
Morris, Phoebe	Composer/Lyricist
Neale, John M.	Lyricist
Newton, John	Lyricist
Nicholson, John	Lyricist
Nicolai, Phillipp	Lyricist
Noble, T. Tertius	Composer
Pace, Kevin G.	Composer
Palmer, H. R.	Lyricist
Parry, Hubert	Composer
Peace, Albert	Composer
Pearson, John V.	Lyricist
Perronet, Edwards	Lyricist
Perry, Janice Kapp	Composer
Petersen, Henry	Lyricist
Phelps, William W.	Lyricist
Pierpoint, Foilliot S.	Lyricist
Praetorius, Michael	Composer
Pratt, Linda	Composer/Lyricist
Pratt, Parley P.	Lyricist
Prichard, Rowland H.	Composer
Ramsay, A. B.	Lyricist
Rankin, Jeremiah E.	Lyricist
Reed, Edith M. G.	Lyricist
Roberts, John	Composer

Robinson, Jason	Composer
Robinson, Robert	Lyricist
Rossetti, Christina	Lyricist
Roth, Monte	Lyricist
Roth, Wally	Composer
Rousseux, John Jacques	Composer
Sachs, Hans	Composer
Sawyer, S. B.	Composer/Lyricist
Sears, Edmund H.	Lyricist
Shaw, Knowles	Lyricist
Sheppard, Franklin L.	Composer
Smart, Henry T.	Composer
Smith, Joseph Jr.	Lyricist
Smith, Marcus L.	Lyricist
Smith, Robb	Lyricist
Snow, Brook C.	Composer/Lyricist
Snow, Eliza R.	Lyricist
Sortomme, Pamela	Composer/Lyricist
Spafford, Horatio G.	Lyricist
Staten, Chad	Composer
Stebbins, George C.	Composer
Steele, Anne	Lyricist
Stephens, Evan	Lyricist
Summers, Sherry	Lyricist
Swain, Joseph	Lyricist
Sweney, John R.	Composer/Lyricist
Taylor, John	Composer
Tallis, Thomas	Composer
Ten Boom, Corrie	Lyricist
Thomas, Toni	Lyricist
Thompson, William L.	Composer/Lyricist
Townsend, Joseph L.	Lyricist
Tuiofu, Diane	Composer
Tullidge, John	Composer
Wade, John F.	Lyricist
Waghorne, W. R.	Composer
Walker, Charles L.	Lyricist
Walker, William	Composer
Walters, Max G.	Composer/Lyricist

Waring, Anna Letitia	Lyricist
Watts, Isaac	Lyricist
Wesley, Charles	Lyricist
Wheelock, Cyrus H.	Lyricist
Williams, Robert	Composer
Willis, Michelle	Composer
Wilson, Hugh	Lyricist
Winkworth, Catherine	Lyricist
Witte, Michelle	Composer/Lyricist
Woodbury, Isaac	Composer/Lyricist
Woodman, Jonathan C.	Composer
Wordsworth, William	Lyricist
Wyeth, John	Composer
Yorgason, Brent	Composer
Young, Michael D.	Composer/Lyricist

Hymns

1 Act Well Thy Part

General Hymns

Michael D. Young

Kevin G. Pace

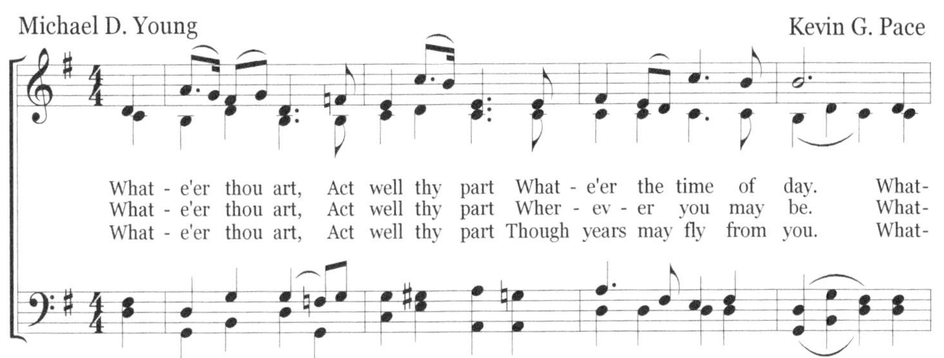
What - e'er thou art, Act well thy part What - e'er the time of day. What-
What - e'er thou art, Act well thy part Wher - ev - er you may be. What-
What - e'er thou art, Act well thy part Though years may fly from you. What-

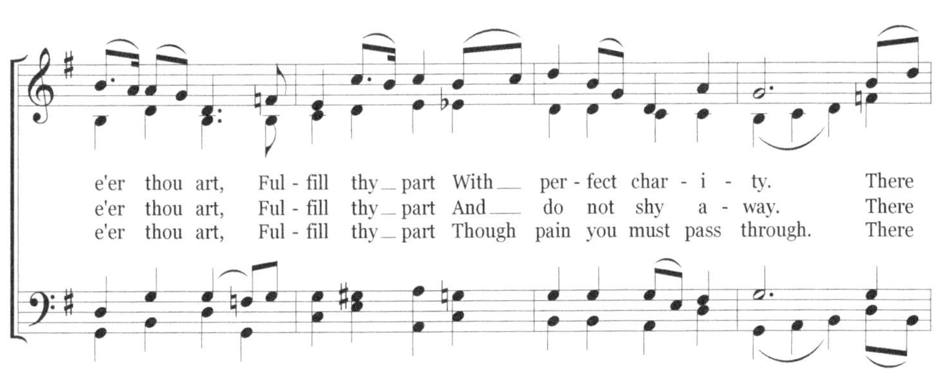
e'er thou art, Ful - fill thy_ part With_ per - fect char - i - ty. There
e'er thou art, Ful - fill thy_ part And_ do not shy a - way. There
e'er thou art, Ful - fill thy_ part Though pain you must pass through. There

is no role so_ low - ly That it es - capes God's gaze. All_
is no deed so_ ti - ny It_ can - not lift a_ No_
is no tear un - count - ed. There is no sigh un - heard. There

peo - ple are im - por - tant That walk in ho - ly ways.
ser - vice is un - need - ed As we seek a heav-'nly goal. What-
is no wound that cuts so deep That it with - stands His word.
e'er thou art Act well thy part with a full and lov - ing heart.

Doctrine and Covenants 64:33

2 A Great and Marv'lous Work Is Ours

General Hymns

Toni Thomas
Diane Tuiofu
A great and marv'-lous work is ours To roll God's king-dom
Be nev-er wear-y of the work, The prize is great, the
As-cend the high and ho-ly mount! Be-hold the en-sign
through the earth! To read-y in these fi-nal hours, Our
prom-ise sure; By oath and cov-e-nant se-cured, We
there un-furled! As righ-teous-ness, from heav-en sent, Joins
hearts, to mag-ni-fy His word. Though now the hour grows dark and fierce,
will ob-tain if we en-dure. Now let us to the task at hand
truth be-low to flood the earth! With cheer-ful mind and read-y hands,
Let not the faith-ful be dis-mayed, For ev-'ry storm of
Bend all our strength and give our best, That we may with the
Press for-ward, hold-ing hope stead-fast Till gath-er-ing from

doubt must cease When dawns that bright, e - ter - nal day.
worth - y stand And now and ev - er claim His rest.
ev - 'ry land, We rise to meet our Lord at last.

Isaiah 29:14
Moses 7:62

3 Abide the Day

General Hymns

Toni Thomas

Diane Tuiofu

3/4
Though now the weight of dark-ness press, Thy light, O Lord, yet pierc-es
Though in this all un-cer-tain hour We know not what to-mor-row
Though now the heav-y bur-dens wear, We meek-ly bear all for Thy
all. Though ha-tred grieve and sin op-press, In Thee we can-not fail nor fall. We
brings, Yet ev-er trust Thy match-less pow'r To bear us up on ea-gles' wings. For
sake. Though sor-rows tempt us to de-spair, We'll seek the sol-ace of Thy grace. Till
shall not fear, we shall not doubt Though storms of op-po-si-tion rage, But
with Thy blood we have been bought And sealed with pro-mise in Thy Name. We'll
tried and pro-ven we are brought In-to Thy rest, no more to stray. We'll
look to Thee in ev-'ry thought, And bright with hope, a-bide the day.
look to Thee in ev-'ry thought, And in Thy peace, a-bide the day.
look to Thee in ev-'ry thought, And in Thine arms, a-bide the day.

Doctrine and Covenants 6:36
Isaiah 40:31

4

General Hymns

All Creation Doth Reverence Thy Majesty, Lord

Laurel Frost

Benjamin Cole

All cre - a - tion doth rev - 'rence Thy maj - es - ty, Lord. For the
Tow - 'ring moun - tains flow down at a blast of Thy breath; Qui - et
What is man? He is less than the dust of the earth. For the
I will fol - low Thy course, as the sun and the moon; I will
stars and the sun and the moon Sing in praise to Thy name with the
val - leys heave up at Thy nod. Storm-y seas be - come calm with a
dust nev - er fails to o - bey; Yea Thy work and Thy glo - ry is
rush to o - bey as the sea. I will bend to Thy will as Thy
heav - en - ly choir, As the plan - ets re - volve to the tune.
glance of Thine eye; Moth - er Earth kneels be - fore Thee, her God.
nur - tur - ing men To be heirs in Thy king - dom one day.
hand - i - work does, That I, too, may bring glo - ry to Thee.

Moses 1:39
Helaman 12:7-8

5

General Hymns

All Things Denote

Michael D. Young
Norma Boyd
All things de - note a ho - ly hand, The
All things de - note a ho - ly mind, All
All things de - note a ho - ly heart, The
All things de - note a ho - ly King. The
won - ders of the sea and land. The
liv - ing things of ev - ery kind, From
splen - dors of all na - ture's art. The
cho - rus - es all crea - tures sing. The
re - gal orb of sun in flight, The
crea - tures too small to be - hold To
maj - es - ty of moun - tains grand, The
praise the el - e - ments af - ford To
stars that come to dance at night.
tow'r - ing red - woods, cen - t'ries old.
can - vas of each fer - tile land.
wor - ship their ce - les - tial Lord.

Alma 30:44

6 All Things Renew

General Hymns

Kevin G. Pace

Michael D. Young and Angie Mae Killian

All things re - new with - in their time, And come in -
All sea - sons come with - in their hour, The glo - ries
All crea - tures find their way back home, Though they have
to their own. The small - est seeds be - come sub - lime,
of the day E - merge to rule with bril - liant pow'r,
strayed a - far. No mat - ter where they fly to roam,
When they are ful - ly grown. The crea - tures
In eve - ning fade a - way. The splen - dors
Birds know from whence they are. They cross the
that in co - coons sleep, Then pri - sm
of the night bring rest, Fore - shad - ow
leagues o - ver sea and land, Re - turn - ing

winged e - merge. Though for a while they slum - ber
the time when, The bril - liant star set in the
to their nest. For some - how they all un - der -
deep, They break on through the verge.
west, With joy shall rise a - gain.
stand, That there they will find rest.

Ecclesiastes 3:1-8

7

Arise, O Glorious Zion

General Hymns

William G. Mills, 1822-1895

Michelle Willis

A - rise, O glo - ri ous Zi - on, Thou joy of lat - ter days, Whom
From Zi - on's stan - dard bear - ers The gos - pel is - sues forth; Their
O hear their proc - la - ma - tion And fly as on the skies! For
Oh, grant, E - ter - nal Fath - er, That we may faith - ful be, And

count - less Saints re - ly on To learn the Sa - vior's ways. A -
mes - sage to the hear - er, "Come gath - er all the earth!" And
souls in ev 'ry na - tion a - wait God's glo - rious prize. Then,
with the righ - teous gath - er, And thy sal - va - tion see! Then

rise and shine in splen - dor A - mid the world's deep night, For
Saints, that mes - sage bring - ing To all the sons of men, With
Zi - on, men shall has - ten To bow be - fore their King; And
with the hosts of heav - en, We'll sing th'im - mor - tal theme: To

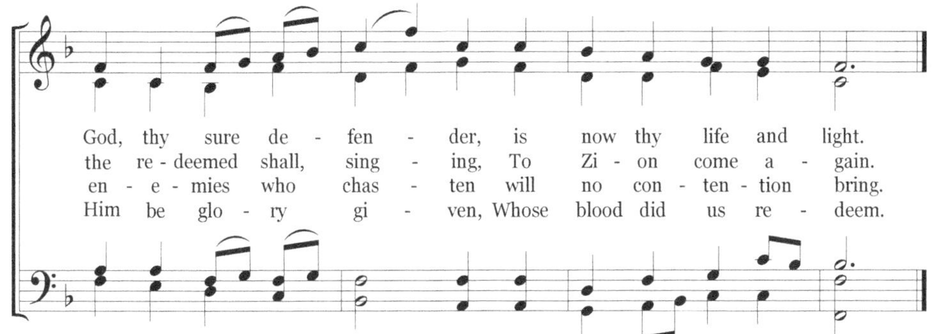
God, thy sure de - fen - der, is now thy life and light.
the re - deemed shall, sing - ing, To Zi - on come a - gain.
en - e - mies who chas - ten will no con - ten - tion bring.
Him be glo - ry gi - ven, Whose blood did us re - deem.

2 Nephi 8:25
Doctrine and Covenants 82:14

As God Has Given Life to Me

Michael D. Young

Kevin G. Pace

As God has giv - en breath to __ me, So may I tes - ti - fy. Of __
As God has giv - en life to __ me, So too may I em - bark, To __
As God has giv - en joy to __ me, So may I sing his praise, With
glo - ries that are yet to __ be, De - scend - ing from the sky, Of
set the souls of man - y __ free, Who lan - guish in the dark. Who
faith that makes the shad - ows flee, And hope that clears my gaze. So
an - cient re - cords now made bright, And tem - ple spires that shine, __ Of __
can - not find the way a - head, Be - cause they do not know, __ The
I shall shine, a bea - con strong, Up - on the high - est hill, __ That
rev - e - la - tion's ho - ly light, And cov - e - nants di - vine.
path that leads to __ liv - ing bread, God's king - dom here be - low.
beck - ons all to __ join in song: The chor - us __ of God's will.

Moses 3:7
John 6:33

9 As Thou Hast Fed the Multitude

General Hymns

Linda Hunzinger

Nora Kay Burnett

As Thou hast fed the mul - ti - tude, oh Sav - ior feed Thou me, The bread of life, the gos - pel truths, which lead me back to Thee
Help me reach forth, ac - cept Thy gift, and grow in - to Thy grace. Bless me to trust Thy words and love, de - sire to see Thy face.
The wa - ter that Thou of - fered to the wo - man at the well, May I drink deep of liv - ing truth, May my life Thy truth tell.

Mark 6:41
Matthew 15:36

Awake, My Soul

Sharlee Glenn

Esther Megargel

My God hath been my
God hath been my
strength through all my days. He's filled me with His love; His name I
strength through all my days. He's filled me with His love; His name I
praise. Why should my soul then lin - ger in de - spair? Why
praise. Give place no more to an - ger sloth, or pride. In
should I weep, and sin my soul en -snare?
God I'll trust; in Him I will a bide.
A -
A
A -
A -

wake, my - soul! Re-
wake my soul! A - wake my soul! No long - er droop in sin.
wake my soul!
wake my soul! A - wake my soul! Re-
joice, my heart!
1
joice my heart! Re – joice my heart! Give praise to God a - gain.
joice, my heart!
2
rit.
My gain.

2 Nephi 4:28
Jacob 3:11

Be Ye Therefore Perfect

Mark R. Fotheringham
Kevin G. Pace
Be ye there - fore per - fect, My Sav - ior said to me, And
Temp - ta - tions all a - round me, My weak - ness - es are clear, But
Show me clear - ly, Fath - er, The path to Thee on high. Help
yet I find that on my own I live im - per - fect - ly.
through a - ton - ing sac - ri - fice He ban - ish - es my fear. Per -
me to know Christ is the On whom I can re - ly.
Each time that I fal - ter, I seek to hide my shame. But
fec - tion still e - ludes me, Though striv - ing year by year. For -
His ex - am - ple guides me, The path of Christ is sure. So
on - ly through con - fes - sion can I seek the Sav - ior's name. Re -
sak - ing sin I turn to God And find Him ev - er near.
step by step I'll fol - low Him And ev - ery test en - dure.

pen - tance is a gift of God From His Be - lov - ed Son. I

hum - bly seek to change my heart And with them both be one.

Matthew 5:48

Beauty for Ashes

Michael D. Young

Michael D. Young

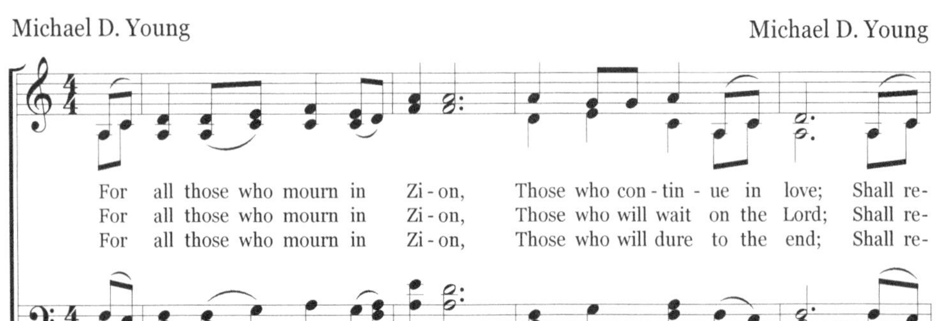
For all those who mourn in Zi - on, Those who con - tin - ue in love; Shall re-
For all those who mourn in Zi - on, Those who will wait on the Lord; Shall re-
For all those who mourn in Zi - on, Those who will dure to the end; Shall re-

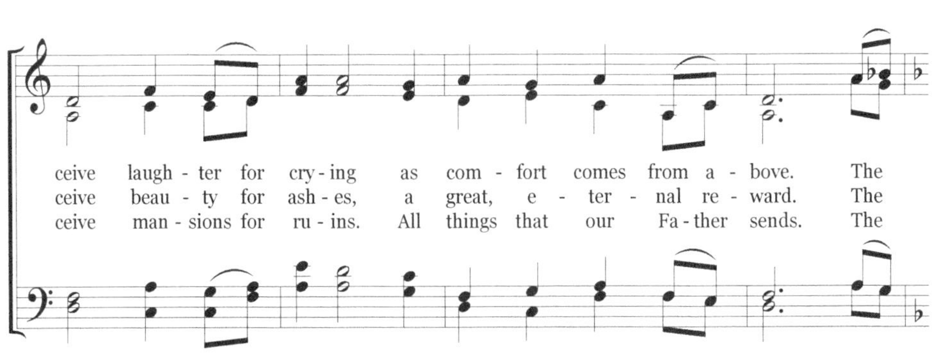
ceive laugh - ter for cry - ing as com - fort comes from a - bove. The
ceive beau - ty for ash - es, a great, e - ter - nal re - ward. The
ceive man - sions for ru - ins. All things that our Fa - ther sends. The

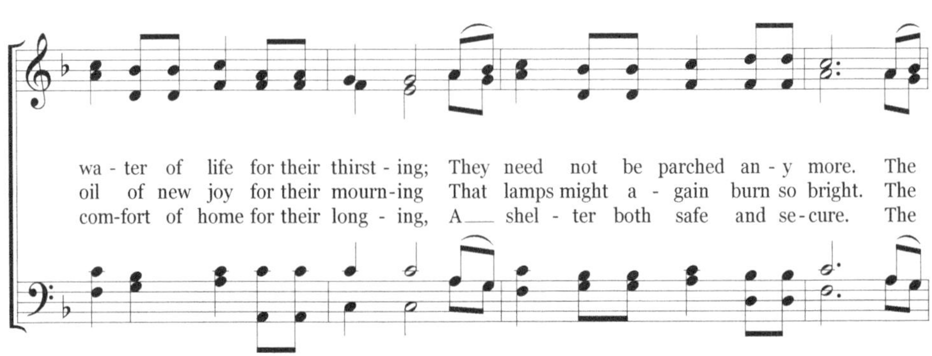
wa - ter of life for their thirst - ing; They need not be parched an - y more. The
oil of new joy for their mourn-ing That lamps might a - gain burn so bright. The
com-fort of home for their long - ing, A ___ shel - ter both safe and se-cure. The

bread of new life for their hun - ger; That will ev - 'ry spir - it re - store.
gar - ment of praise now up - on them In - stead of a dark, hea - vy night. That
smiles of their friends for the lone - ly, A love that is sweet, true and pure.
they may grow in righ - teous - ness, Like trees that God has
plant - ed. Giv - ing glo - ry to the Gar - d'ner, Who ev - 'ry gift has grant - ed.

Isaiah 61:3

13

General Hymns

Beside Still Waters

Gary Croxall
Kathleen Holyoak
Be - side still wa - ters as they flow,
I shall not fear dark e - vil's grasp,
He leads me on, re - stores my soul.
pro - tect - ed by His rod and staff.
He is my shep - herd ev - er - more,
My ta - ble's spread 'midst all my foes,
a - noints my head and fills my cup.
through all my days shall fol - low me,

And though I tread through shad - ows deep,
and I shall dwell in Thine a - bode,

in pas - tures green, I'll rest and sleep.
safe in Thy house, for - ev - er, Lord.

Text © 2015 Gary Croxall
Music © 2015 Kathleen Holyoak

Psalm 23

Blessed Are the Pure in Heart

Michael D. Young — Michael D. Young

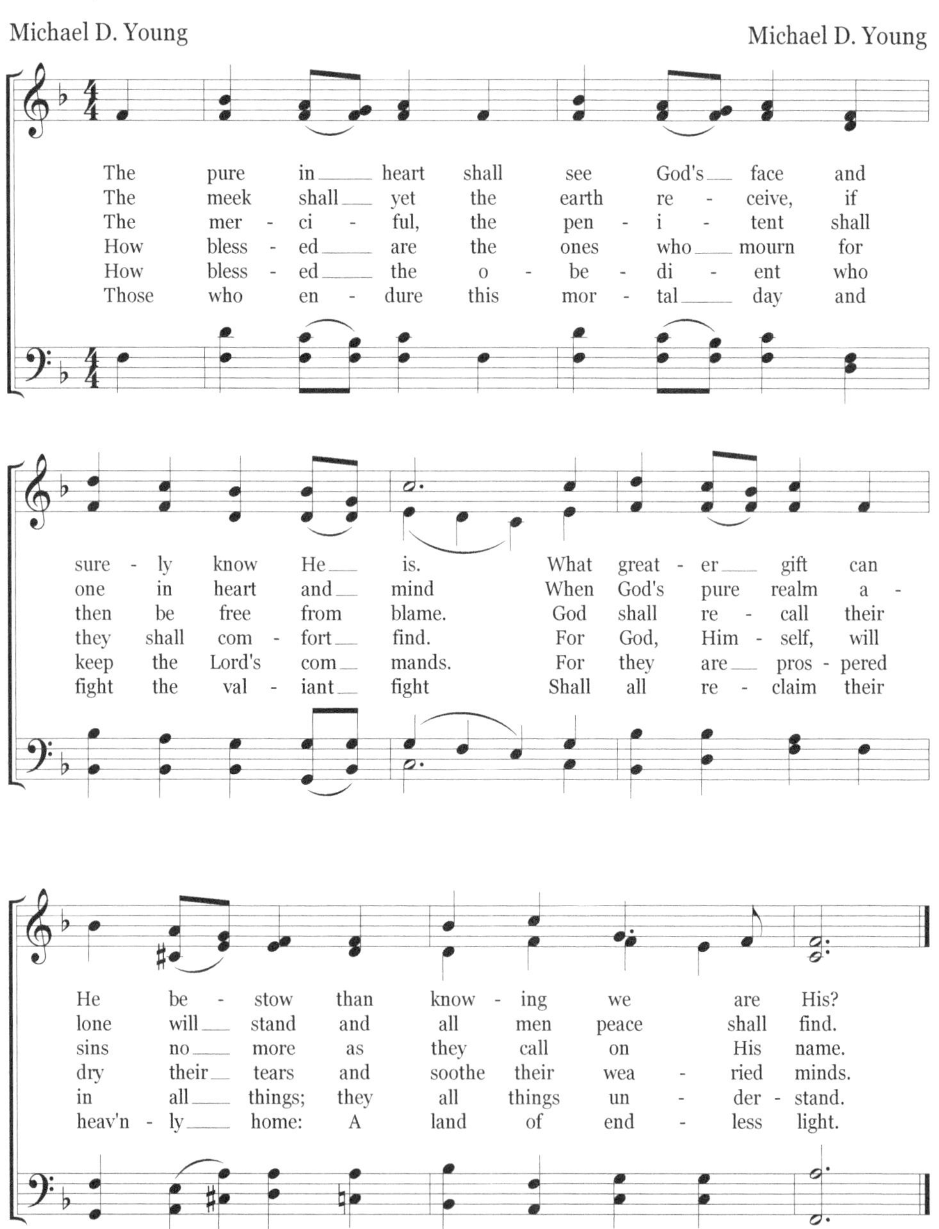
The pure in heart shall see God's face and
The meek shall yet the earth re - ceive, if
The mer - ci - ful, the pen - i - tent shall
How bless - ed are the ones who mourn for
How bless - ed the o - be - di - ent who
Those who en - dure this mor - tal day and
sure - ly know He is. What great - er gift can
one in heart and mind When God's pure realm a -
then be free from blame. God shall re - call their
they shall com - fort find. For God, Him - self, will
keep the Lord's com mands. For they are pros - pered
fight the val - iant fight Shall all re - claim their
He be - stow than know - ing we are His?
lone will stand and all men peace shall find.
sins no more as they call on His name.
dry their tears and soothe their wea - ried minds.
in all things; they all things un - der - stand.
heav'n - ly home: A land of end - less light.

Matthew 5:3-12

15 Blessed, Arise, Your Time Has Come

General Hymns

Michael D. Young

Donna Howard

1.Bless-ed, a-rise, your time has come, God has-tens ev-'ry work to-day. The
2.Bless-ed, a-rise, your time has come, For tem-ples dot the earth to-day. The
3.Bless-ed, a-rise, your time has come, Poor souls still need our help to-day. The
4.Bless-ed, a-rise, your time has come, Our hearts shall be re-fined to-day. Through

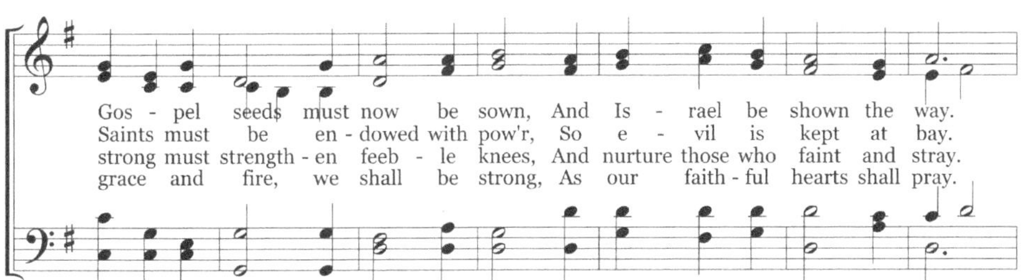
Gos-pel seeds must now be sown, And Is-rael be shown the way.
Saints must be en-dowed with pow'r, So e-vil is kept at bay.
strong must strength-en feeb-le knees, And nurture those who faint and stray.
grace and fire, we shall be strong, As our faith-ful hearts shall pray.

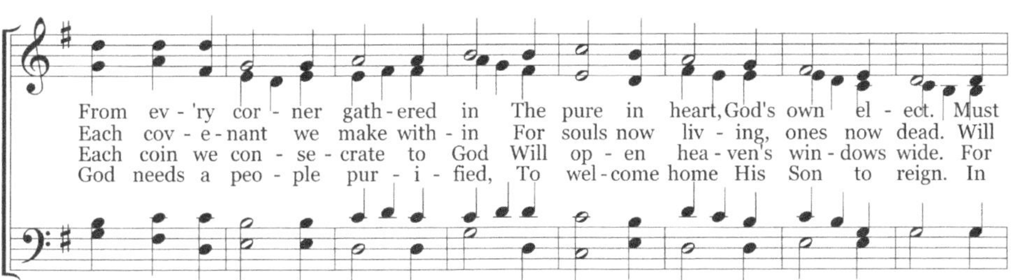
From ev-'ry cor-ner gath-ered in The pure in heart, God's own el-ect. Must
Each cov-e-nant we make with-in For souls now liv-ing, ones now dead. Will
Each coin we con-se-crate to God Will op-en hea-ven's win-dows wide. For
God needs a peo-ple pur-i-fied, To wel-come home His Son to reign. In

leave be-hind a world of sin, And ev-'ry world-ly care re-ject.
make the veil of heav-en thin, as we a-rise where an-gels tread.
as we share the wealth a-broad, Our ev-'ry need will be supp-lied.
whom He spi-rit may a-bide, And keep them clean from ev-'ry stain.

2 Nephi 1:23
Moroni 10:31

16 By Faith

General Hymns

Michael D. Young

Norma Boyd

By faith we come be - fore God's face, And kneel be - fore His throne. For
By faith we see with clear - er sight Be - yond our mor - tal eyes. Faith
By faith we tap the ho - ly source Of Liv - ing Wa - ter sweet. By
all who run life's wea - ry race. We do not strive a - lone, For
lends to us God's ho - ly might, Like cur - ren - cy that buys The
faith we feast on ev - 'ry course Of heart - y, ho - ly meat. By
faith will bring God's pow'r to all Who take it as their shield, And
faith and trust with - in our souls To move a - head de - spite The
faith our hun - ger will be filled, That we may lack no By
ev - 'ry foe of truth will fall When faith's sure sword they wield.
ob - sta - cles that block our goals, The dark - ness of the night.
faith the fear of death is stilled. We trust what lies in store.

Alma 32
Ether 12

17

General Hymns

By Lives of Charity

Michael D. Young

Norma Boyd

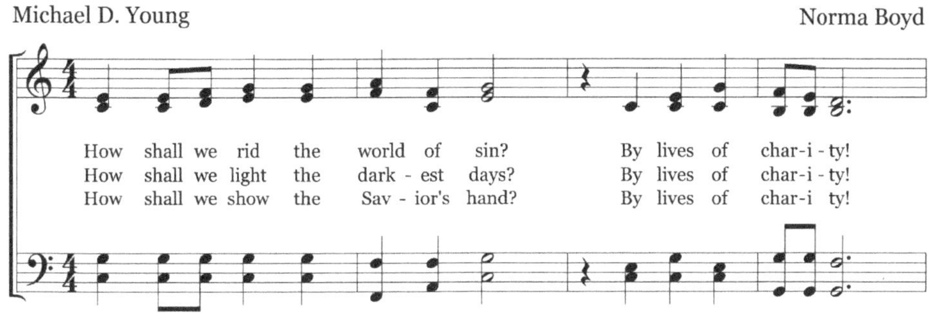
How shall we rid the world of sin? By lives of char-i-ty!
How shall we light the dark-est days? By lives of char-i-ty!
How shall we show the Sav-ior's hand? By lives of char-i ty!

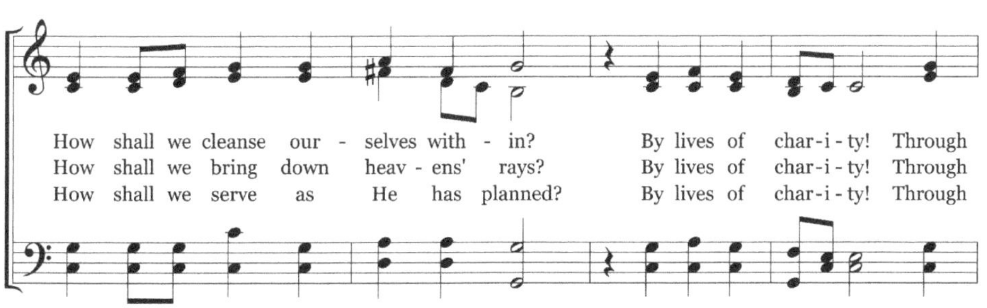
How shall we cleanse our-selves with-in? By lives of char-i-ty! Through
How shall we bring down heav-ens' rays? By lives of char-i-ty! Through
How shall we serve as He has planned? By lives of char-i-ty! Through

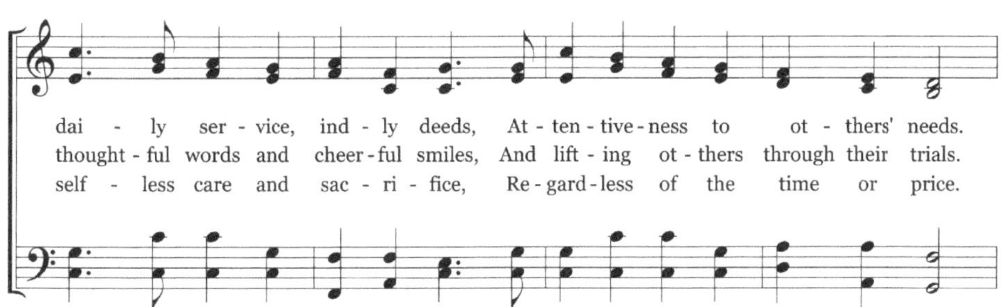
dai-ly ser-vice, ind-ly deeds, At-ten-tive-ness to ot-thers' needs.
thought-ful words and cheer-ful smiles, And lift-ing ot-thers through their trials.
self-less care and sac-ri-fice, Re-gard-less of the time or price.

How shall we rid the world of sin? By lives of char - i - ty!
How shall we light the dark - est days? By lives of char - i - ty!
How shall we show the Sav - ior's hand? By lives of char - i - ty!

1 Corinthians 13:1-4
Moroni 7:1, 44-47

18

Can Ye Feel So Now?

Michael D. Young

Michael D. Young

My friends, if you've been taught to sing the
Have you been stripped of all your pride? Can
If you were called this hour to die Can
song of re - deem - ing love
ye feel so now?
ye feel so now?
I ask, I ask, you
And free of en - vy,
To meet the judge - ment
fer - vent ly: Can ye feel so now?
void of strife. Can ye feel so now?
from on high. Can ye feel so now?
Can ye feel so now? Can ye feel so now?

Alma 5

Choose You This Day

Annette W. Dickman

Annette W. Dickman

Choose you this day whom you will serve, Choose you this day whom to fol-low. As for
3rd Time To Coda
me and mine the choice is clear. We will serve the Lord our God.
Choose you this day the path you'll walk, Wheth-er the broad one or nar-row. As for
me and mine the course is set. We will hold the i-ron rod.
Man-y will try to
Man-y will mock and

lead us a - stray. We can find safe - ty in one nar - row way. Our
not un - der - stand. We can be true and fol - low His plan, And
Sav - ior has called, if we fol - low we'll know the right way to go.
we with our fam - 'lies will kneel at His throne e - ter - nal - ly home.
Coda
God. We will serve the Lord, our God.

Mark 6:41
Matthew 15:36

Christ the Lord is Ever Near

Mark R. Fotheringham

Kevin G. Pace

Tu - mults in the lat - ter days, Tem - pests teach - ing men to pray
Ev - er since the days of old Man - y proph - ets have fore - told
All our hopes and all our fears, All our dreams through all the years
To the God of pow'r and might, Help - ing us to choose the right.
He'll re - turn, the King of Kings, Bring - ing heal - ing in His wings. Stand
Lead us all to that great day When our dear Sav - ior comes a - gain.
fast! The righ - teous need not fear. Christ the Lord is ev - er near.

D&C 84:88

21 Come Join the Ranks of Zion's Grand Army

General Hymns

Joseph Smith, adapted

Kevin G. Pace

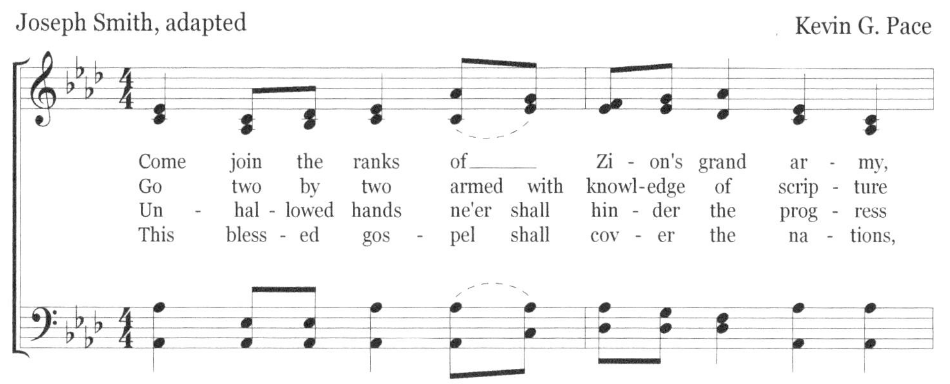
Come join the ranks of Zi - on's grand ar - my,
Go two by two armed with knowl-edge of scrip - ture
Un - hal - lowed hands ne'er shall hin - der the prog - ress
This bless - ed gos - pel shall cov - er the na - tions,

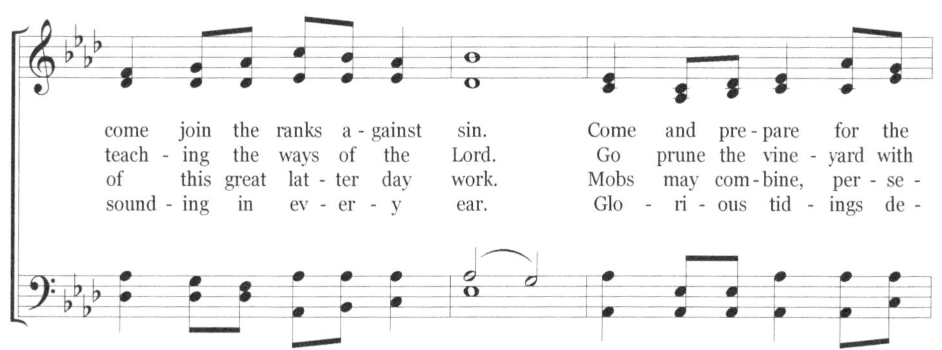
come join the ranks a - gainst sin. Come and pre - pare for the
teach - ing the ways of the Lord. Go prune the vine - yard with
of this great lat - ter day work. Mobs may com - bine, per - se -
sound - ing in ev - er - y ear. Glo - ri - ous tid - ings de -

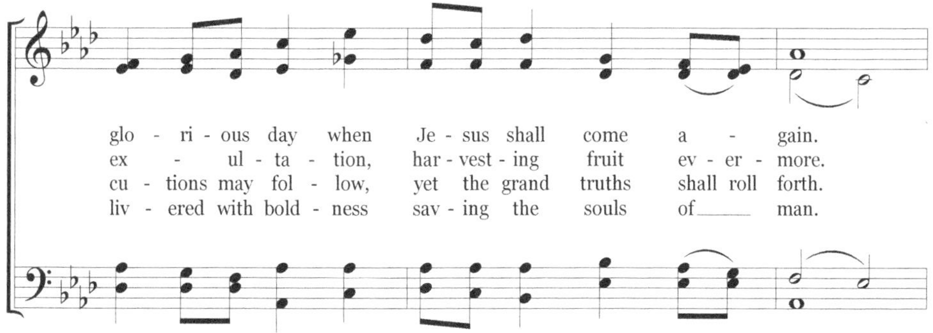
glo - ri - ous day when Je - sus shall come a - gain.
ex - ul - ta - tion, har - vest - ing fruit ev - er - more.
cu - tions may fol - low, yet the grand truths shall roll forth.
liv - ered with bold - ness sav - ing the souls of man.

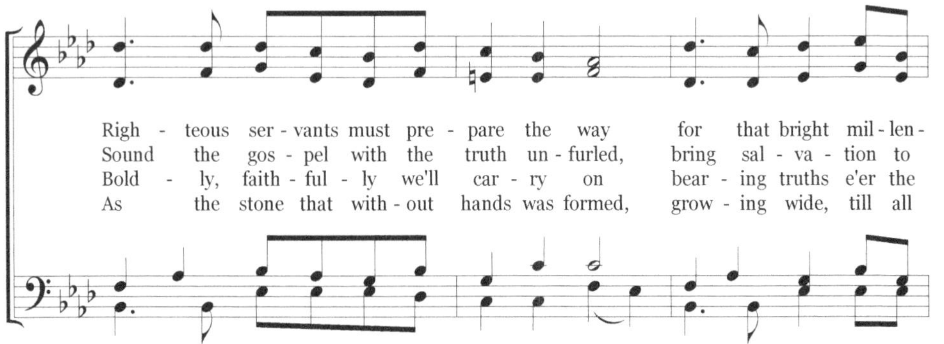
Righ - teous ser - vants must pre - pare the way for that bright mil - len -
Sound the gos - pel with the truth un - furled, bring sal - va - tion to
Bold - ly, faith - ful - ly we'll car - ry on bear - ing truths e'er the
As the stone that with - out hands was formed, grow - ing wide, till all

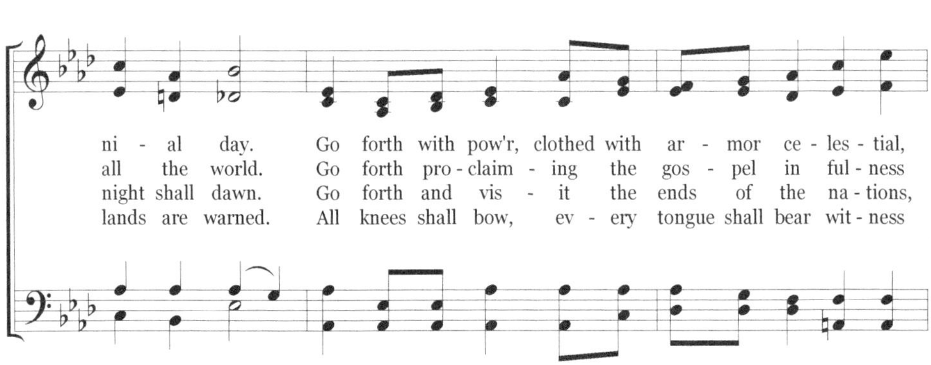
ni - al day. Go forth with pow'r, clothed with ar - mor ce - les - tial,
all the world. Go forth pro - claim - ing the gos - pel in ful - ness
night shall dawn. Go forth and vis - it the ends of the na - tions,
lands are warned. All knees shall bow, ev - ery tongue shall bear wit - ness

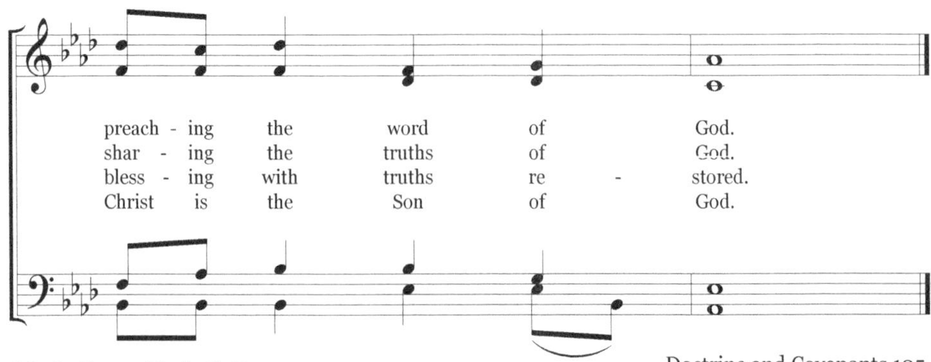
preach - ing the word of God.
shar - ing the truths of God.
bless - ing with truths re - stored.
Christ is the Son of God.

Doctrine and Covenants 105

22 Come to the Mountain of the Lord

General Hymns

Nathan Howe

Nathan Howe

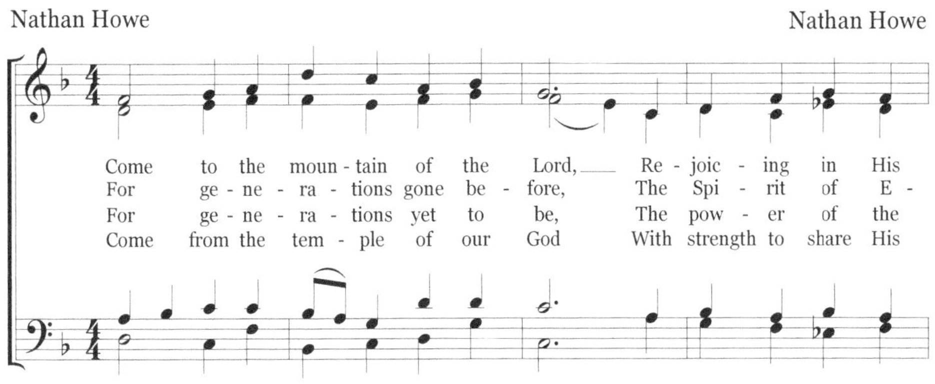
Come to the moun - tain of the Lord, Re - joic - ing in His
For ge - ne - ra - tions gone be - fore, The Spi - rit of E -
For ge - ne - ra - tions yet to be, The pow - er of the
Come from the tem - ple of our God With strength to share His

pres - ence; Hun - gry for wis - dom from on high,
li - jah Calls to per - form the work of love;
priest - hood Seals us with God in cov - e - nant.
gos - pel, Bring - ing the world in - to His fold.

Come to the moun - tain of the Lord,
Come to the moun - tain of the Lord,
Come to the moun - tain of the Lord,
"Come to the moun - tain of the Lord!"

Clothed in His name and glo - ry.
Hearts tur - ning to your fa - thers.
Where fam - 'lies are for - ev - er.
An - gels are round a - bout you.

Isaiah 2:2-3

23

General Hymns

Come to the Temple

Annette W. Dickman

Annette W. Dickman

Come to the tem - ple, the house of the Lord.
Come to the tem - ple and go forth to serve, to
Come to the tem - ple of glo - ri - ous light.
Come to the tem - ple, the Lord's ho - ly place.
Come be His guest and be taught of His word.
share His gos - pel with all on the earth.
Come wor - ship hum - bly in robes of pure white.
Come par - take of His mer - cy and grace.
Come feel His peace and His ho - li - ness with - in.
Come be en - dowed with His pow - er from on high and
Come and be sealed an e - ter - nal fam - i - ly,
Come and re - ceive rev - e - la - tion to your soul.
Come be His child and re - turn to Him a - gain.
cov - 'nant pro - tec - tion in His watch - ful eye.
bound by His priest - hood for all e - ter - ni - ty.
Come and com - mune with that God who makes you whole.

Mark 6:41
Matthew 15:36

Crown after Cross

Nathan Howe

Nathan Howe

Light af - ter dark - ness, gain af - ter loss,
Sheaves af - ter sow - ing, sun af - ter rain,
Near af - ter dis - tant, gleam af - ter gloom,
Strength af - ter weak - ness, crown af - ter cross;
Sight af - ter mys - ter - y, peace af - ter pain;
Love af - ter lone - li - ness, life af - ter tomb;
Sweet af - ter bit - ter, hope af - ter fears,
Joy af - ter sor - row, calm af - ter blast,
Af - ter long ag - o - ny, rap - ture of bliss:
Home af - ter wan - der - ing, praise af - ter tears.
Rest af - ter wear - i - ness, sweet rest at last.
Right was the path - way lead - ing to this.

Doctrine and Covenants 112:14
Doctrine and Covenants 76:108

25
General Hymns

Endurance

Nathan Howe
Nathan Howe
My_ Sav - ior is the Lord of out - stretched arms,
My_ Sav - ior is the Lord of heal - ing hands,
My Sav - ior knows the pains of ev - 'ry heart,
In - vit - ing all to_ look to_ Him and live.
Though hea - ling may not_ hap - pen right a - way.
For_ He has felt the_ sting of ev - 'ry sin.
To_ reach Him, I must stand a - gainst the storms,
To_ work and_ wait and strive for all we can
He_ prom - is - es, if I will do my part,

En - cour - raged by the peace I know He'll give.
Will stretch our souls un - til the per - fect day.
He'll lift me up and lead me home a - gain.
O Fa - ther, wilt thou help me to en - dure
The fire that will re - fine and make me pure!

Matthew 24:13
Doctrine and Covenants 14:7

Enduring to the End

Michael D. Young
Michael D. Young
I know some - day with all cer - tain - ty I will
My loved ones I will take with me, all en -
see my ris - en Lord. I hope to see His smil - ing face and
cir - cled in God's love. We will re - main a fam - i - ly in
hear his ten - der word. My depth of joy and
that bright world a - bove. We'll grow and prog - ress e -
grat - i - tude will be too much to com - pre - hend. I now look for - ward
ter - nal - ly, in a life that has no end. I now look for - ward

to that day en - dur - ing to the end. My
to that day en - dur - ing to the end.

Lord, help me en - dure! Lord, help me

to be pure. I now look for - ward

to that day, en - dur - ing to the end.

Matthew 24:13
Doctrine and Covenants 14:7

Enjoy the Journey

Rick Graham

Rick Graham

Life is meant to be a jour-ney, as we trav - el on the roads,
We can make the world much bet - ter with our smiles and help-ing hands.
When our jour - ney is con - clud - ed and we take our fi - nal breath,
Shar - ing love un - feigned and kind, with all of those who do not know.
We can al - ways make a diff'r - ence to those who don't un - der - stand.
Do not mourn for us, our pass - ings are but jour - neys be - yond death.
En - joy ev - 'ry mo-ment! En - joy ev - 'ry day! Smile, and help each
oth - er On their jour - ney's way.

1 Nephi 8:24
2 Nephi 31:20

28

General Hymns

Every Hymn I Bear toward Zion

Marcus L. Smith

Dan Montez

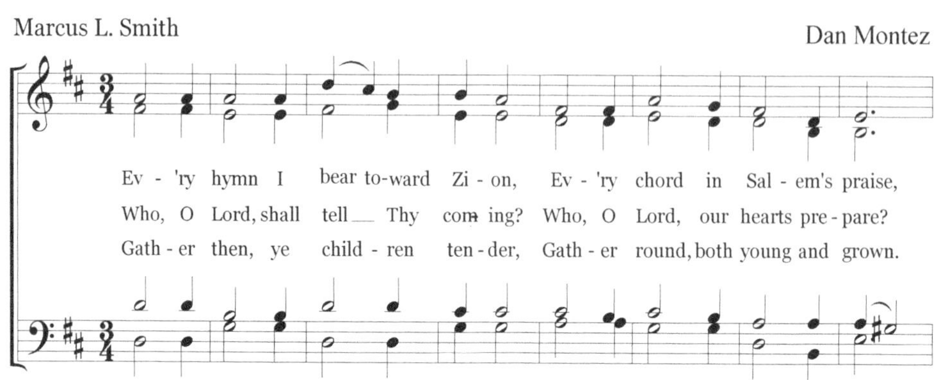

Ev - 'ry hymn I bear to-ward Zi - on, Ev - 'ry chord in Sal - em's praise,
Who, O Lord, shall tell Thy com ing? Who, O Lord, our hearts pre - pare?
Gath - er then, ye child - ren ten - der, Gath - er round, both young and grown.

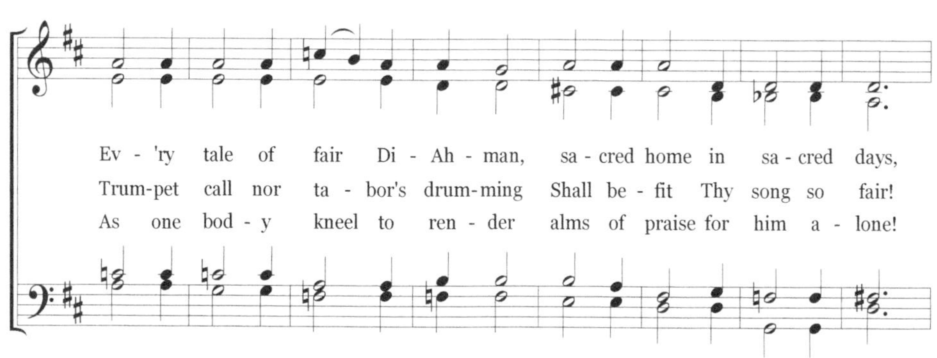

Ev - 'ry tale of fair Di - Ah - man, sa - cred home in sa - cred days,
Trum-pet call nor ta - bor's drum-ming Shall be - fit Thy song so fair!
As one bod - y kneel to ren - der alms of praise for him a - lone!

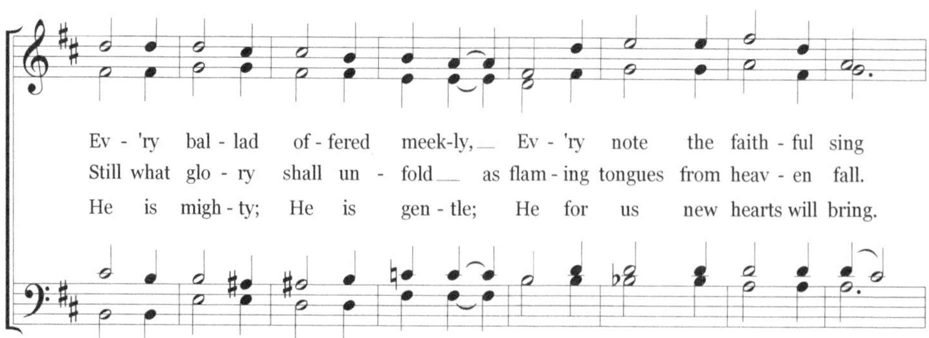

Ev - 'ry bal - lad of - fered meek-ly, Ev - 'ry note the faith - ful sing
Still what glo - ry shall un - fold as flam - ing tongues from heav - en fall.
He is migh - ty; He is gen - tle; He for us new hearts will bring.

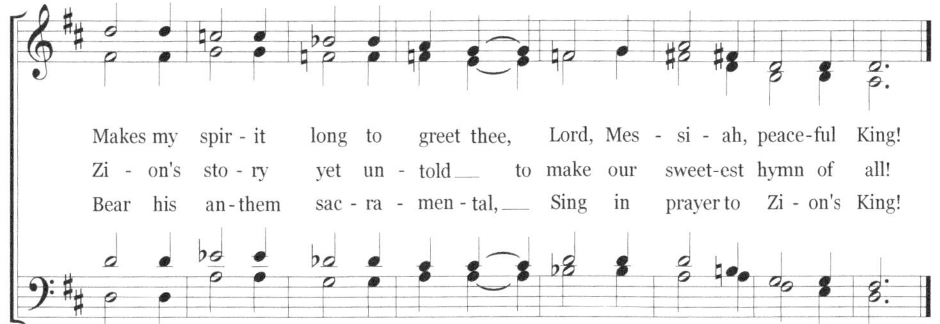
Makes my spir - it long to greet thee, Lord, Mes - si - ah, peace-ful King!
Zi - on's sto - ry yet un - told to make our sweet-est hymn of all!
Bear his an-them sac - ra - men - tal, Sing in prayer to Zi - on's King!

Isaiah 35:10

29 Father, Hear Us Lift One Voice

General Hymns

Hyrum Mead
Rosemary Mead
Fa - ther, hear us lift one voice, For
With one spir - it, wilt Thou fill Us
All Thou gav - est to Thy Son May
in one gos - pel we re - joice!
with one mind to do Thy will,
we re - ceive as we are one.
In our Lord has all be - come One
One in heart, work, and pur - pose, One
And through - out e - ter - ni - ty. We'll
hope, one joy, one sal - va - tion.
bod - y framed in per - fect - ness.
dwell as one, our God with Thee.

John 17:22
Timothy 2:5

30 Fullness Restored

Kevin G. Pace

Mark G. Fotheringham

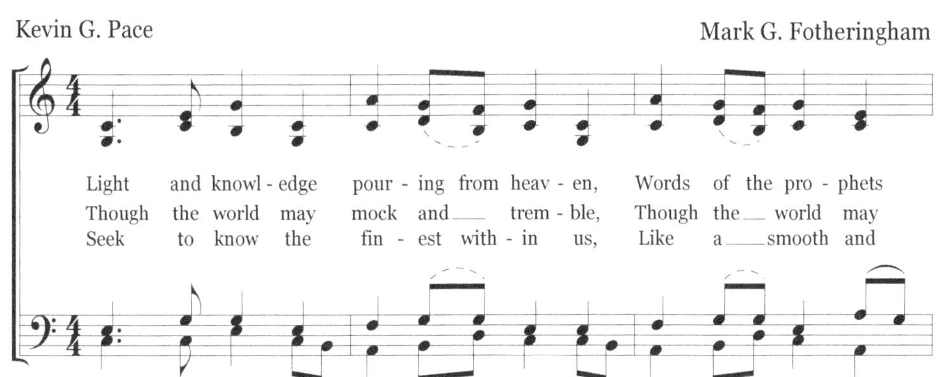
Light and knowl - edge pour - ing from heav - en, Words of the pro - phets
Though the world may mock and trem - ble, Though the world may
Seek to know the fin - est with - in us, Like a smooth and

all are ful - filled. Firm foun - da - tions root - ed in doc - trine
go a - stray, Help us be Thy cov - en - ant peo - ple,
shin - ing stone. Try to see as God tru - ly sees us;

For the full - ness to be re - vealed. A - ges past, the
Keep us in the nar - row way. Christ has suf - fered
Seek to know as we are known. Once, our hearts were

gos-pel was cor-rup - ted Till a boy im - plored, (boy im-plored.)
for___ all___ man - kind. We will not be swayed, (not be swayed.)
filled with__ dark - ness. Now let joy be shown, (joy be shown.)

Light and knowl - edge pour - ing from heav - en,
Though the world may mock and___ trem - ble,
Seek to know the fin - est with - in us;

For the full - ness to be re-stored.
Keep us in the nar - row___ way.
Seek to know as we are___ known.

Daniel 2:44

God Looks upon the Heart

Michael D. Young
Kevin G. Pace
God's love looks on the heart And not up - on our face. It
God's love looks on the mind And not up - on the frame. It
God's love looks on the soul And not what holds it here. Its
does not ask for wealth, It warms, a sweet em - brace. It pre-
smi - les on the kind And warms them like a flame. It in-
touch can those con - sole Who trem - ble, sick with fear. It's a
pares hearts for good. It soft - ens bits of stone. Its speech is un - der-
vig - or - ates all. It fills with new vi - sion. It lifts us when we
strong, sure re - sort. It an - chors in the waves. It of - fers firm sup-
stood Its voice is sim - ply known.
fall, It guides each de - ci - sion.
port. It ev - 'ry crea - ture saves.

1 Samuel 16:7

32 Have Thine Own Way, Lord

General Hymns

Adapted from Adelaid A. Pollard
Jared Bernotski
Have Thine own way, Lord! Have Thine own way! Thou art the
Have Thine own way, Lord! Have Thine own way! Search me and
Have Thine own way, Lord! Have Thine own way! Wound - ed and
Have Thine own way, Lord! Have Thine own way! Hold o'er my
pot - ter, I am the clay. Mold me and make me af - ter Thy
try me, Mas - ter to - day! Whit - er than snow, Lord, wash me pure
wea - ry, help me I pray! Pow - er, all pow - er, sure - ly is
be - ing ab - so - lute sway. Fill with Thy Spir - it till all shall
will, while I am wait - ing yield - ed and still.
now, as in Thy pres - ence hum - bly I bow
Thine! Touch me and heal me, Sav - ior di - vine!
see Christ on - ly, al - ways, liv - ing in me!

Music © 2015 Jared Bernotski

Isaiah 64:8
Helaman 3:35

33 Hearken to the Prophets

General Hymns

Monte Roth

Wally Roth Arr. by Kathleen Holyoak

Heark - en to the
Heark - en to the
Heark - en to the
proph-ets of old and lat - ter days. Lis - ten to their
proph-ets, whose mar - tyred souls cry out, "March - ing t'ward His
proph-ets. Their faith and hopes em - brace. Pray with hum - ble
mes-sage and em - u - late their ways. Search the words of Je - sus who
glo - ry," their tes - ti - mo - nies shout! Jus - ti - fy their suf-f'ring Re -
spir - it to share their sa - cred place. Live by their ex - am - ple, His
sac - ri - ficed His life, Teach - ing man by pre - cept to
live their faith ex - pressed. Trust our lov - ing Sav - ior, for
gos - pel to pro - claim. Know there's life e - ter - nal through

con-quer fear and strife. Live by love and kind - ness. Re-pent of all thy
this we shall be blessed. We're His spir - it chil - dren, who made the glo-rious
Je - sus's ho - ly name. Heark-en to the prompt-ings of His pro-phet-ic
sins. Help thy friends and neigh - bors; there char - i - ty be -
choice; Life as mor - tal be - ings, we hailed with great re -
voice. Speak-ing through our con - science, to guide us in our
gins. O - ver-come temp - ta - tions that test our hu - man ways.
joice. Hear His words of prom - ise to lead us home once more.
choice. Urg - ing us to fol - low where His dis - ci - ples trod.
Tread the straight and nar - row; in - vite God's no - ble praise.
To His ho - ly king - dom where - in we dwelt be - fore.
March - ing with the faith - ful whose foot - steps seek - eth God.

Amos 3:7
Revelation 10:7

34

He Is My Cornerstone

General Hymns

Lyle Hadlock

Lyle Hadlock

When I'm a - lone and can - not see, Je - sus is there watch - ing o - ver
sad, con - fused and lost, my Sav - ior knows what my pain doth
knows both you and me. He un - der - stands what our eyes can't

me. When I kneel down with my heart bare, Je - sus is
cost. He un - der - stands my ev - ery woe. Yes, Je - sus
see. He's con - stant in His per - fect love. He's our re -

1,2
3
ver - y close I feel Him near. When I feel
knows my pre - cious soul. My Lord, He
deem - ing Lord, born to save us. He is the

rit.
Sav - ior of all men! He gave His life for all my sins! And all He asks of you and
me is, "Live my words and come fol - low me." When I am
lost and all a - lone my Je - sus is my cor - ner - stone.

3 Nephi 5:13
Luke 14:33

35
General Hymns

Help Is Wanted

Rick Graham | Rick Graham

unison
Help is want - ed, the gos - pel shared each day. Help is want-ed, I'll lis - ten and o - bey. I will be an ex - am - ple to my friends, Show - ing them that Je - sus is my friend.
Help is want - ed, I'll show a gen - tle hand. Help is want-ed, I'll help you un - der - stand That right choic - es you make can pave the way For your good in all you do and say.
Help is want - ed we'll live the gos - pel, true. Help is want-ed, we'll read the scrip-tures too. We will pray to our Fa - ther, and to see, as His Dis - ci - ples, we will al - ways be.

John 12:26
Mosiah 2:18

36 Holy Temples

Rick Graham

Rick Graham

Ho - ly tem - ples, sa - cred build - ings, cov - 'nants made and fam - 'lies bind.
Bap - tized for those who can't do them, hop - ing they em - brace the Plan.
En - dow - ment with prom - ised bles - sings are all ours, this prom - ise sure,
We are sav - iors on Mount Zi - on when our fam - 'ly's work is done.
Place of wor - ship, place of learn - ing, of our Heav'n - ly Fa - ther, kind.
Giv - ing choic - es to ac - cept it; gos - pel of the Son of Man.
Seal - ing pow - ers, ex - al - ta - tion, if we all can but en - dure.
Bind - ing all as fam - 'ly u - nits link - ing all, for - get - ting none.
Come back to His ho - ly tem - ples; come back of - ten. Don't de - lay!
Washed, a - noint - ed roy - al lin - eage bles - sings of e - ter - nal worth.
Or - din - an - ces for the liv - ing, or - di - nanc - es for the dead.
Ho - ly tem - ples, sa - cred build - ings, cov - 'nants made and fam - 'lies bind.
Learn of His love to all man - kind, hear well what the Spir - it says.
Sa - cred gar - ments placed up - on us, re - mind - ers for all on earth.
This im - por - tant work will not end, Till the Fa - ther's word is said.
Place of wor - ship, place of learn - ing, in these tem - ples we will find.

Doctrine and Covenants 138:54

37 How Great Is Our Lord

Robb Smith
Chad Staten
How great is our Lord! He reigns in glo - ry
Au - thor of love, He pens His mes - sage
Yet shad - ow clouds my soul's pure prais - es
His love a - bounds 'midst trial and sor - row.
Oh Fa - ther, may I live to serve, and
o'er the sons of men. He
on each star of night. His
to the Light of Men. A -
Else, how shall man grow? Christ
bend like son to sire. En -
lead - eth us when Him we trust: our
rays of truth bid dark - ness flee, and
bide I must, though Him I trust that
ran - somed us. He paid our debt. He
grave Thy name from day to day on

God who rules in heav'n.
fill the world with light.
dawn will shine a - gain.
all things passed be - low.
my poor heart with fire.

6. My God, my heart sings out Thy praises! Nor can mortal tell
How wondrous is our Lord and King who came to earth to dwell!

1 Nephi 1:14

38 How Sweet the Spirit's Beckoning

General Hymns

Hyrum Mead

Rosemary Mead

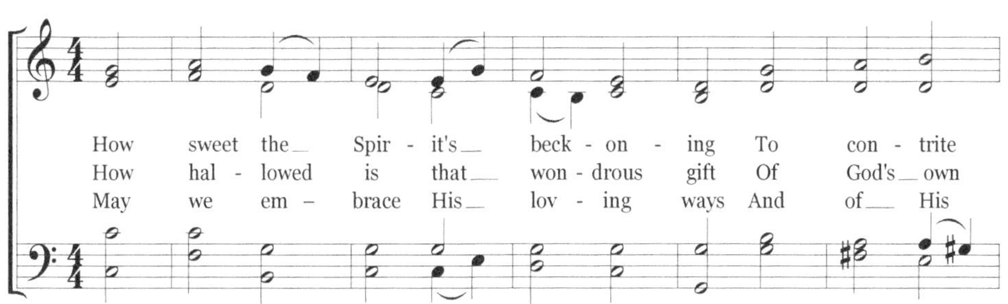
How sweet the Spir - it's beck - on - ing To con - trite
How hal - lowed is that won - drous gift Of God's own
May we em - brace His lov - ing ways And of His

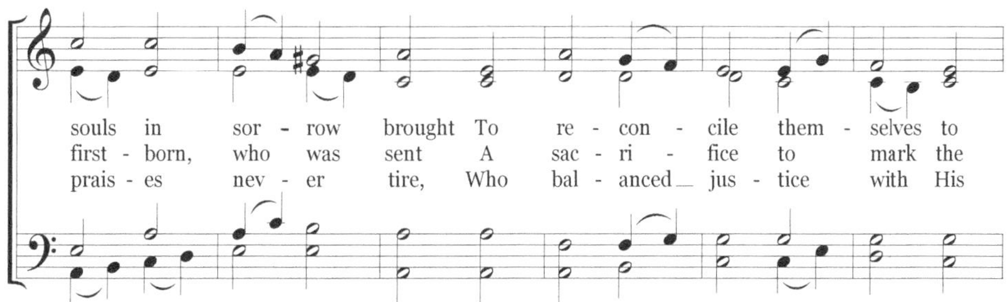
souls in sor - row brought To re - con - cile them - selves to
first - born, who was sent A sac - ri - fice to mark the
prais - es nev - er tire, Who bal - anced jus - tice with His

God And count their van - i - ties as naught.
way For all who seek Him and re - pent.
love And pu - ri - fies our souls with fire.

Ephesians 2:18
Jacob 4:11

39

How Sweet to Me!

Michael D. Young — Michael D. Young

Sav-ior, Sav-ior, how sweet Thy soul to me!
Sav-ior, Sav-ior, how sweet Thy works to me!
Sav-ior, Sav-ior, how sweet Thy words to me!
Sav-ior, Sav-ior, how sweet Thy love to me!
Thy words up - on my heart im - press.
The Son who from the Fa - ther sent,
Com - pel - ling me to grasp the rod,
My soul from sin He shall re deem.
Mak - ing calm my deep dis - tress. Ev - 'ry breath breathes bless - ed - ness!
Walked the path and called "Re - pent!" Sow - ing love where - e'er He went.
Taste the fruit, and feel God's love, Feast on gifts sent from a - bove
Through my trials, His hope shall gleam. Peace and mer - cy, like a stream.
How sweet Thy soul to me!
How sweet Thy works to me!
How sweet Thy words to me!
How sweet Thy love to me!
div.

Alma 32:42
Psalms 104:34

I'll Follow Jesus Christ

Gary Croxall Kathleen Holyoak

I'll fol - low Je - sus Christ Wher - ev - er I may go. Through
I'll fol - low Je - sus Christ. He'll take me home a - gain. I'll
each and ev - ery choice, He'll guide and help me grow. I'll choose to do what's right. O-
lis - ten to His voice, Come quick - ly un - to Him. I'll stay close by His side, Re-
bey the Lord of all. I'll walk with-in the light And heed the Sav - ior's call.
main with - in His sight. I'll fol - low Je - sus Christ And walk with - in His light.

Matthew 24:13
Doctrine and Covenants 14:7

41
General Hymns

In the Savior's Name

Mark R. Fotheringham

Kevin G. Pace

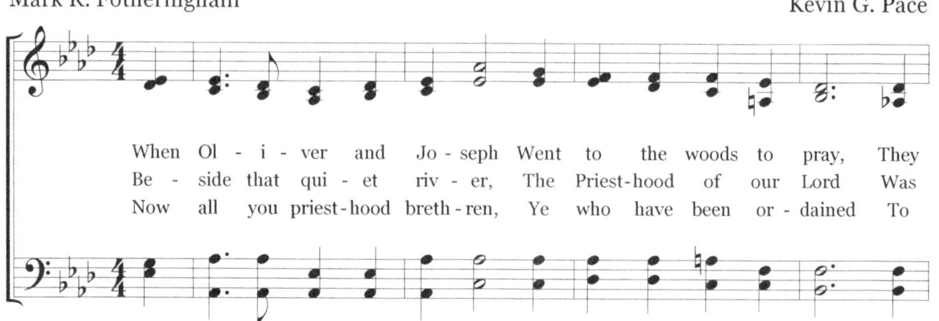
When Ol - i - ver and Jo - seph Went to the woods to pray, They
Be - side that qui - et riv - er, The Priest-hood of our Lord Was
Now all you priest-hood breth - ren, Ye who have been or - dained To

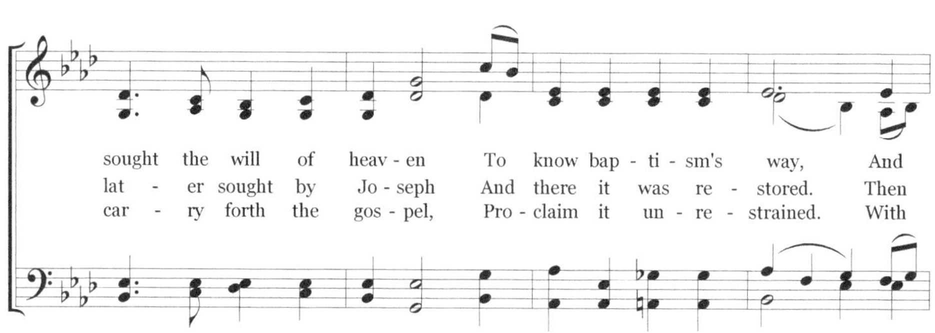
sought the will of heav - en To know bap - ti - sm's way, And
lat - er sought by Jo - seph And there it was re - stored. Then
car - ry forth the gos - pel, Pro - claim it un - re - strained. With

there the an - cient Bap - tist Gave them pow'r to do the same, Re -
through the con - fir - ma - tion Of___ Pe - ter, John, and James, They were
gifts be - stowed up - on you Heal the sick and mend the lame, But re -

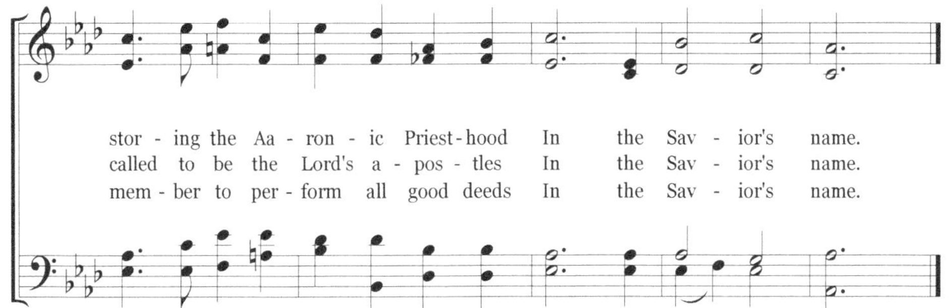
stor - ing the Aa - ron - ic Priest-hood In the Sav - ior's name.
called to be the Lord's a - pos - tles In the Sav - ior's name.
mem - ber to per - form all good deeds In the Sav - ior's name.

2 Nephi 31:21

I Will Follow Christ

Laurel R. Frost

Henry T. Smart, adapted

unison
The doc - trine of the Sav - ior brings joy e - ter - nal - ly I
ask God to for - give me, re - pent - ing day by day. The
bap - tized in the wa - ter and cov - 'nant to be true. I
priest-hood I'm con - firmed to re - ceive the Ho - ly Ghost. I'll
place my faith in Je - sus, who gave His life for me. Have
Sav - ior's pow'r and mer - cy will take my sins a - way.
want to please the Sav - ior in all I say and do.
lis - ten to His whis - p'rings each time I make a choice.
faith in Christ the Sav - ior, re - pent and be bap-tized. Re - ceive the Ho-ly Spir - it.
1, 2, 3.
4.
Yes, I will fol - low Christ.
I
I'm
By
I will fol - low Christ!

Arrangement © 2015 Laurel R. Frost

Articles of Faith 1:4

43

General Hymns

I Worship God

Norma Boyd

Norma Boyd

I wor-ship God with all my heart, Sing prais-es to His name.
I wor-ship God with all my heart, For ev-'ry-where I see
I wor-ship God with all my heart, And with my ac-tions, too.
It was be-cause of love for us That to this earth He came.
Ev-i-dence real that He still reigns With love and maj-es-ty.
I'll show Him that my love is real In ev-'ry-thing I do.
Here to suf-fer un-told grief And pain that knew no bounds, That
Moun-tains grand and wa-ters clear Re-mind me that He cares. The
Com-fort-ing the griev-ing heart And eas-ing oth-ers' hurts Will
low-ly sin-ners He might help To win ce-les-tial crowns.
joy that comes from new-born life Still says to me He's there.
show Him that I fol-low Him In more than just my words.

I wor - ship God with all my heart.

2 Nephi 25:29
Doctrine and Covenants 19:16-19

44

Jesus Is My Savior

General Hymns

Norma Boyd

Norma Boyd

Je - sus is my Sav - ior. He is the Son of God. His
Je - sus is my Broth - er, His love for me is real. He
Je - sus, my Re - deem - er, re - moved death's aw - ful sting. Re -
As I drink the wa - ter, I feel His love for me. I
love for me is ev - i - dent in ev - 'ry - thing He taught. He
of - ten lifts and com - forts me. My gap - ing wounds He heals. He
stor - ing joy for bit - ter - ness, He makes the filth - y clean. He
think of all the blood He shed while in Geth - sem - a - ne, And
gave Him - self a sac - ri - fice and paid for ev - 'ry sin.
laid down on the al - tar and did it wil - ling - ly.
brings me hope and heal - ing, re - mov - ing fi - ery darts.
as I eat the bro - ken bread, I pon - der on His life,
Je - sus suf - fered ag - o - ny, my pre - cious soul to win.
There He suf - fered rid - i - cule and hor - rid ag - o - ny.
Je - sus longs to mend my soul and peace and love im - part.
Giv - en up on Cal - va - ry. He paid an aw - ful price!

Je - sus made it pos - si - ble for me to live a - gain.
Je - sus bled from ev - 'ry pore and gave His life for me.
He wants me to come to Him, so He can heal my heart.
Je - sus thought my pre - cious soul was worth the sac - ri - fice.

Luke 22:44
Mosiah 3:7

Let Me, Oh Lord, Lead Others to Thee

Ryan Larsen — Ryan Larsen

Past pain we seek Thee, through trial we trod,
Through mist we wan - der, cring - ing we cry,
Al - pha, O - me - ga, Song of the Saints,
Ev - er and al - ways clo - ser to God.
While clos - er near - er to Thee we fly.
Heal - er of heart - aches and all com - plaints,
Light of our Lov - ing Ru - ler of
Life of our liv - ing King of the
The might - y Mast - er, our Prince of
right Guid - ing in day time, hold - ing at
kind, Heal - ing the bod - y eas - ing the
Peace, With Thy a - ton - ing all sor - rows

night. Let me, oh Lord, lead oth - ers to Thee,
mind. Let me, oh Lord, lead oth - ers to Thee,
cease. Let me, oh Lord, lead oth - ers to Thee,
as Thou hast giv - en com - fort to me.
as Thou hast giv - en new hope to me.
as Thou hast giv - en all things to me.

Doctrine and Covenants 18:15

46 Let Us Bow before His Throne

Mark R. Fotheringham

Kevin G. Pace

When in doubt we question, our faith a sand-y shore,
When the soul is an-guished, the spir-it cries in pain.
When in joy we pros-per, and glo-ry we pro-claim,
Ho-ly words as-sure us, and our Rock is there once more.
Then the Sav-ior heals us, and re-stores our faith a-gain.
Help us to be hum-ble, nev-er to for-get Thy name.
Nev-er will He a-ban-don, nor leave us all a-lone. The
Nev-er will He a-ban-don, nor leave us all a-lone. The
Nev-er let us a-ban-don, the way that Thou hast shown. The

King of Kings, He knows all things.
King of Kings, He knows all things. Let us bow be-fore His throne.
King of Kings, He knows all things.

Doctrine and Covenants 76:93
Doctrine and Covenants 88:104

47 Lord, Accept Our Offering

General Hymns

Nathan Howe
Nathan Howe
Lord, ac - cept our of - fer - ing Giv - en to the meek.
Lord, ac - cept our hon - est tithe; May Thy king - dom grow.
Lord, ac - cept our of - fer - ing Of a bro - ken heart.
Mag - ni - fy our of - fer - ing: Pu - ri - fy our hands.
May the spir - it of our fast Nour - ish those who seek.
O - pen heav - en's win - dows wide; Bless us here be - low.
Make our spir - its more con - trite; Sav - ing truth im - part.
Con - se - crate our dai - ly work To Thy might - y plan.

Doctrine and Covenants 108:9
Doctrine and Covenants 59:14

Lord, May I Not Forget

Michael D. Young
Norma Boyd
Lord, may I not for - get That Thou all things hast made, That
Lord, may I not for - get That Thou dost nev - er sleep. Thy
Lord, may I not for - get That Thou art in con - trol, So
Lord, may I not for - get That Thou wilst bring us back, The
we are in Thy debt, But should not be dis - mayed. For
eye is on me yet When my eyes pour and weep. For
that when oth - ers fret Thou wilt my heart con - sole. For
plan that Thou hast set Will make up where we lack. It
Thou dost free - ly give Of Thy a - bun - dant grace, And
Thou dost not for - sake The faint - ing and the lost, For
Thou dost hold us all A - loft with - in Thy hand. With -
is Thy whole de - sign To bless Thy daugh - ters, sons, Through
quick - ly will for - give All those who seek Thy face.
they, too may par - take And think not on the cost.
out Thee we would fall. With Thee, we un - der - stand.
that fire to re - fine Us in - to wor - thy ones.

Alma 30:44

49 Love Is a Daily Choice

General Hymns

Michael D. Young

Norma Boyd

Love is a dai - ly choice: The soft tone of your voice;
Love is a dai - ly choice: In oth - er's good re - joice;
Giv - ing the great - er part; And serv - ing with your heart; En -
Re - pair each lit - tle wrong To forge a friend-ship strong; For -
gag - ing with your mind; Com - mit - ting to be kind;
give an - oth - er's sin, Sin - cere - ly look with - in;
A sweet and self - less view In ev - ery - thing you do.
Re - lieve an - oth - er's pain And let your love re - main.

John 13:34-35

50 May Thy Daystar Rise in Me

Toni Thomas

Diane Tuiofu

As sun and moon roll on their wings And by Thy ho - ly
In dark - ness, still, Thy light tran - scends, Though dark - ness doth not
When I have taught mine eye to be Kept sin - gle to Thy
To - mor - row dawns that per - fect day, When care and shad - ow

reck - on - ing, Do give their light by night and day, So,
com - pre - hend. Thy child - ren walk by noon - day light Through
maj - es - ty, Then shall my soul be filled with light, And
fade a - way. I'll see my Sav - ior face to face, And

Fa - ther, may my life por - tray Thy glo - ry and Thy
all the dark and fear - ful night. Dear Fa - ther, I Thy
for - mer dark - ness flee my sight. Pray, Fa - ther, hear my
live for - ev - er in His grace. For quick - ened then I

maj - es - ty; Oh, may Thy Day - star rise in me!
child would be! Oh, may Thy Day - star rise in me!
hum - ble plea; Oh, may Thy Day - star rise in me!
long to be. Oh, may Thy Day - star rise in me!

2 Peter 1:19
Doctrine and Covenants 88

Memorial Day

Rick Graham

Joyce Kilmer

The bu - gle ech - oes shrill and sweet,
The ros - es blos - som white and red
A - bove their wreath - strewn graves we kneel,
May we, their grate - ful chil - dren, learn
In shin - ing rank on rank ar - rayed
but not of war it sings to - day.
on tombs where wea - ry sol - diers lie;
they kept the faith and fought the fight.
their strength, who lie be - neath this sod,
they march, the le - gions of the Lord;
The road is rhyth - mic with the feet
flags wave a - bove the hon - ored dead,
Through fly - ing lead and crim - son steel,
Who went through fire and death to earn
He is their Cap - tain un - a - fraid,

of men at arms who come to pray.
and mar - tial mu - sic cleaves the sky.
They plunged for free - dom and the right.
at last the ac - co - lade of God.
the Prince of Peace, who brought a sword.

Alma 29:12
Psalms 116:7

52 Moroni's Golden Trumpet

General Hymns

Donald Ashdown

Franklin D. Ashdown

Mo - ro - ni's gold - en trum - pet sounds E - li - jah's mes - sage clear From
Ho - san - nas loud we sing to Thee, on this, Thy ho - ly day. As
With - in these ho - ly tem - ple walls we con - se - crate to Thee, Our
Let earth-bound man lift up his head, leave world - ly cares be - hind. Ex -
Help us, O Lord, pure lives to live, from mor - tal sins be free, That

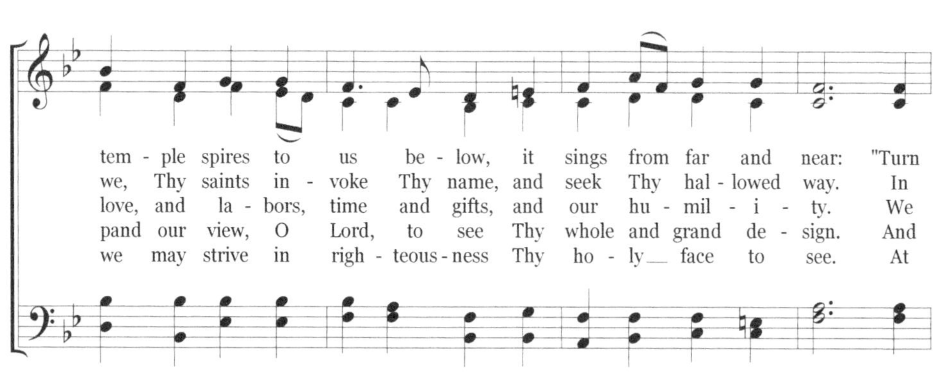
tem - ple spires to us be - low, it sings from far and near: "Turn
we, Thy saints in - voke Thy name, and seek Thy hal - lowed way. In
love, and la - bors, time and gifts, and our hu - mil - i - ty. We
pand our view, O Lord, to see Thy whole and grand de - sign. And
we may strive in righ - teous - ness Thy ho - ly face to see. At

hearts of fa - thers to their kin and those of kin - dred birth Lest
ser - vice free and love un - feigned we toil for those long dead That
bow our heads and kneel to Thee, and with our tongues con - vey The
wrap in fam - 'ly cir - cles dear sal - va - tion's warm em - brace To
al - tars pure, with hearts con - trite, we cov - e - nant with Thee That

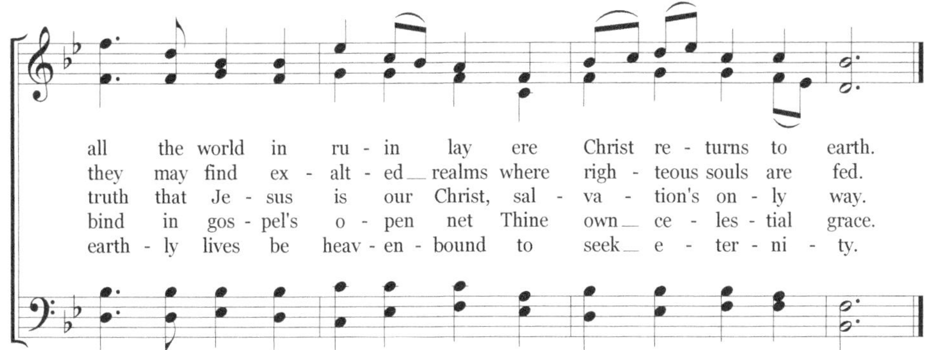
all the world in ru - in lay ere Christ re - turns to earth.
they may find ex - alt - ed realms where righ - teous souls are fed.
truth that Je - sus is our Christ, sal - va - tion's on - ly way.
bind in gos - pel's o - pen net Thine own ce - les - tial grace.
earth - ly lives be heav - en - bound to seek e - ter - ni - ty.

Doctrine and Covenants 42:6
Doctrine and Covenants 88:103

53 My Joy Is in Thy Service, Lord

General/Relief Society Hymns

Hyrum Mead

Rosemary Mead

Thoughtfully (♩.=54)
1. My joy is in ___ thy
2. I give my heart ___ to
3. Help me to lead ___ thy
4. How great my joy ___ in

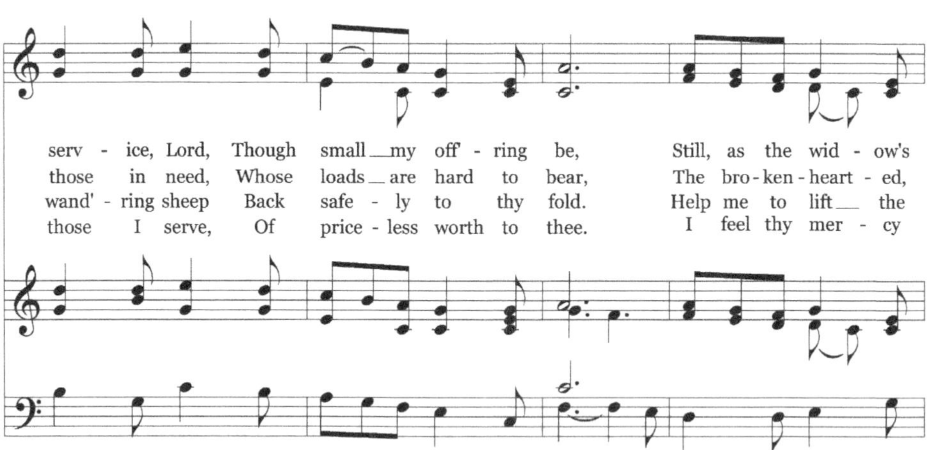
serv - ice, Lord, Though small ___ my off' - ring be, Still, as the wid - ow's
those in need, Whose loads ___ are hard to bear, The bro - ken - heart - ed,
wand' - ring sheep Back safe - ly to thy fold. Help me to lift ___ the
those I serve, Of price - less worth to thee. I feel thy mer - cy

mite, may mine Be found of worth to thee.
weighed with grief, The lone - ly in des - pair.
beat - en soul By - passed a - long the road.
and thy love For them, and e - ven me.

Alma 27:18
Philippians 2:17

54 My Life Is But a Weaving

General Hymns

Florence M. Alt

Felix Mendelssohn, arr. Michael D. Young

My life is but a weav - ing be - tween my God and me. I
Not till the loom is si - lent And the shut - tles cease to fly Will
He knows, He loves, He cares; Noth - ing this truth can dim. He
can - not choose the col - ors, He weav - eth stead - i - ly. Oft -
God un - roll the can - vas And re - veal the rea - son why. The
gives the ver - y best to those who leave the choice to Him. My
times He weav - eth sor - row; And I in fool - ish pride, For -
dark threads are as need - ful In the weav - er's skill-ful hand, As
life is but a weav - ing Be - tween my God and me. I
get He sees the up - per and I the un - der - side.
the threads of gold and sil - ver in the pat - tern He has planned.
can - not choose the col - ors, He weav - eth stead - i - ly.

Doctrine and Covenants 122:7-9

55
General Hymns

No Matter What I May Achieve

Michael D. Young — Michael D. Young

No mat - ter what I may a - chieve, It pales when I con - sid - er Thee, Who paints the heav - ens day and night And fills the world with warmth and light And lends His life to fowl and beast And ev - 'ry man from great to least.
No mat - ter what my wealth or fame, It can - not rise to the ac - claim That does from ev - 'ry na - tion rise And ech - oes from the vault - ed skies, That still is sung since years un - known And ris - es end - less to Thy throne.

My works all van - ish in a breath Be -
My own re - nown is i - dle, naught To

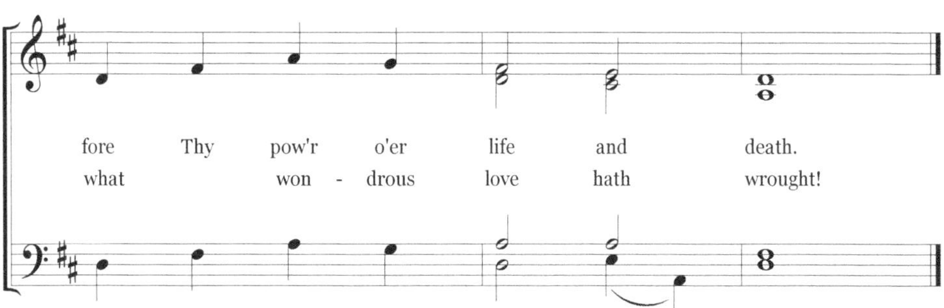
fore Thy pow'r o'er life and death.
what won - drous love hath wrought!

Mosiah 2:25

56

No Purer Love

Michael D. Young
Norma Boyd
No pur-er love could be ex-pressed, Or ev-er to us shown,
No pur-er love has been re-vealed, Was nev-er man-i-fest
No pur-er love will we then know Than when we see His face,
No mo-ment could be called more blessed Than that when Christ a-toned.
Than when Christ in the Gar-den kneeled And God on high ad-dressed.
For sure-ly then our tears will flow As we ac-cept His grace.
Praise now the gift of sweet-est love That Christ on us be-stows, Sus-
Praise now the gift of self-less love That Christ a-greed to make, That
Praise now the gift of pres-ent love That we will then par-take, For
tain-ing as the sun a-bove, The ten-der-ness He shows.
draws us to our home a-bove If we our sins for-sake.
this we know both here, a-bove, His love will not for-sake.

Moroni 7:47

57 Now Is the Hour for Faith, Not Fear

General Hymns

Toni Thomas

Annette Dickman

Now is the hour___ for faith, not fear: We toil a - gainst the
This is a day___ for hope, not doubt: In mat - ters great and
Now is the time___ our love is proved, when noth - ing seems as -

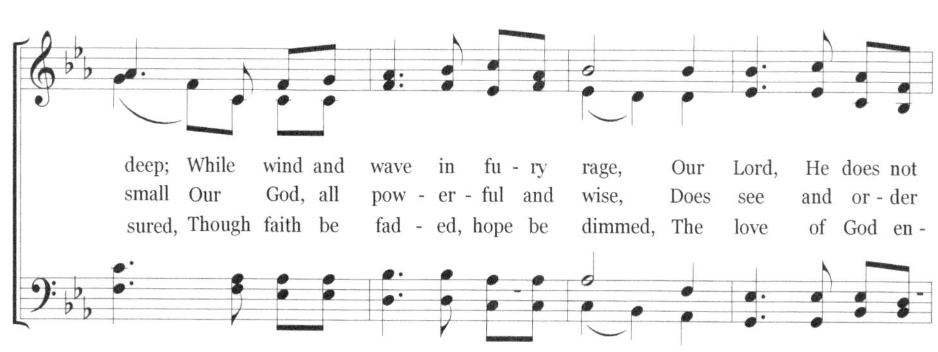
deep; While wind and wave in fu - ry rage, Our Lord, He does not
small Our God, all pow - er - ful and wise, Does see and or - der
sured, Though faith be fad - ed, hope be dimmed, The love of God en -

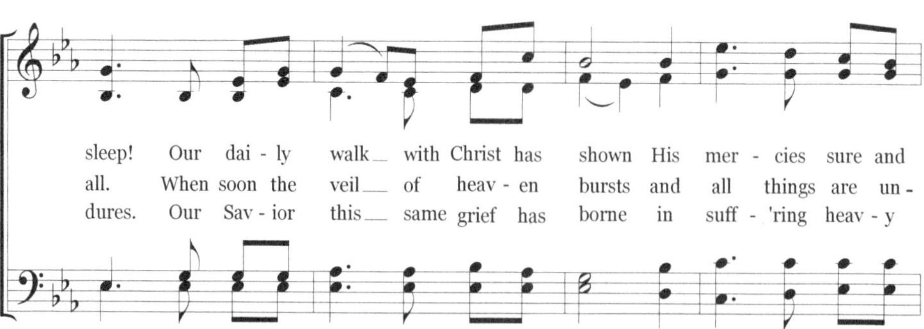
sleep! Our dai - ly walk___ with Christ has shown His mer - cies sure and
all. When soon the veil___ of heav - en bursts and all things are un -
dures. Our Sav - ior this___ same grief has borne in suff - 'ring heav - y

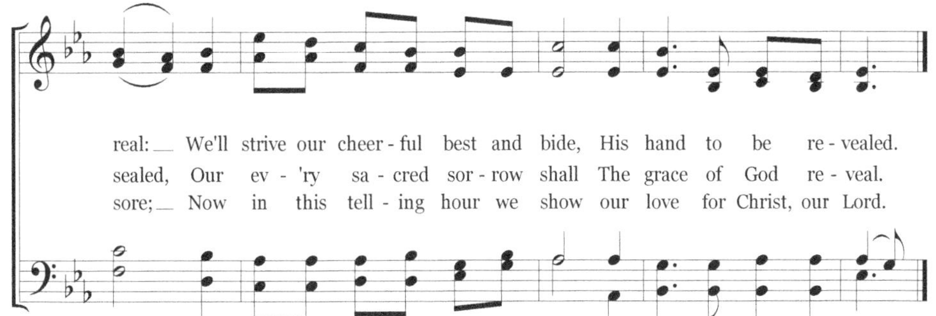
real: We'll strive our cheer - ful best and bide, His hand to be re - vealed.
sealed, Our ev - 'ry sa - cred sor - row shall The grace of God re - veal.
sore; Now in this tell - ing hour we show our love for Christ, our Lord.

2 Timothy 1:7
Romans 8:15

Oh Jesus, Savior of Mankind

Randall D. McNeely
Kimberly N. McNeely
Oh Je - sus, Sav - ior of man - kind, We
Oh Je - sus, Sav - ior of the world, Thy
Oh Je - sus, Thy ho - ly name be praised. In
Oh Je - sus, may we Thy hands be. For
Oh Je - sus, when Thy work is done, And
thank Thee for Thy plan di - vine, For mak - ing Thy sweet gos - pel
ban - ner now has been un - furled. It waves for all the world to
grat - i - tude this hymn we raise, And ask Thee through this prayer in
all man - kind on land and sea, By mak - ing Thy sweet gos - pel
all the saints with Thee are one, May we find joy and rest with
known, Which leads us to the way back home.
see. And says to "Come, fol - low me."
song, To help us move Thy work a - long.
known, Which guides Thy pre - cious chil - dren home.
Thee, And praise Thy name e - ter - nal - ly.

2 Peter 3:18
Doctrine and Covenants 20:4

59 Oh, to Have Been in Kirtland

General Hymns

Mark R. Fotheringham

Kevin G. Pace

Oh, to have been in Kirt - land When the veil was o - pened wide, To
Oh, to have been in Kirt - land See - ing Mo - ses there ap - pear, Com-
Oh, to have been in Kirt - land, vi - sions glo - ri - ous to see, To
see the Sav - ior stand - ing in the air, and there a - bide. To
mit - ting keys to gath - er Those of Is - rael, far and near. E -
know the res - to - ra - tion Of the gos - pel makes men free. The
hear the great Je - ho - vah, Rush - ing wat - ers as His voice, Pro -
li - as and E - li - jah There pro - claimed a bless - ing sure For
Lord will meet His ser - vants In the House that bears His name, There

claim - ing sins for - giv - en: "Lift up your heads and re - joice."
fu - ture gen - er - a - tions And for their fa - thers be - fore.
pour - ing out a bless - ing On - ly the righ - teous can claim.
The tem - ple was ac - cept - ed as a ho - ly house of God.
The saints would be per - fect - ed By the cov - e - nants they made,
And if we still are wor - thy To com - mand - ments giv - en there,
En - dow - ing saints with pow - er To spread His word a - broad.
And reach - ing out to oth - ers Who'd lost their way or strayed.
Our tem - ples will be a ref - uge From all our trou - ble and care.

Doctrine and Covenants 110

60 Our Birth Is But a Sleep

William Wordsworth — Kevin G. Pace

Our birth is but a sleep and a for - get - ting. (for - get - ing.) The
soul that ris - es with us, our life's star, (our life's star,) Hath
had else-where its set - ting and com-eth from a - far: Not in en -
tire for - get - ful-ness, and not in ut - ter na - ked-ness, But

trail - ing clouds of glo - ry do we come from God, from God, who is our from

God who is our home. Heav-en lies a - bove us in our in - fan - cy.

Music © 2015 Kevin G. Pace

1 Nephi 1:14

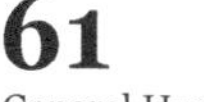

Prayer of Thanks

Gary Croxall

Kathleen Holyoak

Praise the Lord who reigns a - bove, Wor - ship Him in truth and love. Rev - 'rence Him, all ye that live. A prayer of thanks to Him we give. He hath made both star and sky,

God, who formed both sea and shore, All the waves that surge and roar; Thine ex - is - tence these at - test In north and south and east and west. Ston - y mount or ver - dant dale,

Sun and moon that soar on high.
Gen - tle wind or clouds that sail;

All His gran-deurs us a - maze. Come sing to Him in joy - ous praise.
Beau - ti - fy this place we live. A prayer of thanks to Thee we give.

Psalms 26:7
Psalms 100:4

62

Raise Your Voices to the Lord

General Hymns

Evan Stephens

Esther Megargel

Raise your voic - es to the Lord,
giv- ing! Let our song
Ye who here have heard His word. As we part, His praise pro -
Still our joy and praise pro - long, Un - til here we meet a -
1
2
claim, Shout thanks - giv - ing to His name.
gain To re - new the Shout thanks - glad re - frain.

Psalm 100

Rejoice as Saints of the Latter Days

Dianne Killburn

Jana McGettigan

Be - lov - ed Fa - ther, we u - nite In true de - vo - tion for the right, That
In - crease our tes - ti - mo - ny, Lord, Of Thy pure gos - pel now re - stored. Di-
We ded - i - cate our lives to Thee; Sus - tain - ing home and fam - i - ly. A
faith - ful ser - vants we may be, Clothed in robes of char - i - ty.
rect our steps by ho - ly light, As we seek Thy path a - right. Re-
cov - 'nant ple, ho - ly race; Blessed by Thy e - ter - nal grace.
joice! Re-joice! Come let us sing, In prais - es to our Lord and King. Re-
joice, and let our works give praise, As Saints of the lat - ter days.

2 Nephi 32:9

64 Rejoice, Rejoice, Rejoice

Ryan Larsen

Ryan Larsen

Re joice! Re - joice! Re - joice! We
Re - pent! Re - pent! Re - pent! This
A - men! A - men! A - men! Let
Re - joice! Re - joice! Re - joice! Re - joice!
Re - pent! Re - pent! Re - pent! Re - pent!
A - men! A - men! A - men! A - men!
shout in hap - py voice! In glo - rious song we
mes - sage He has sent from proph - ets' writ - ings,
sing the hosts of men! The tongues of an - gels
shout His praise as this our might - y an - them raise in
long now past, and now raised up a - gain at last, so
sing the song, then let us join their heav'n - ly throng, so
these the glo - ri - ous lat - ter days, Re - joice! Re - joice! Re -
haste and to the Word hold fast: Re - pent! Re - pent! Re -
let us sing for - ev - er long, "A - men! A - men! A -

joice! Re - joice, we sound through - out the earth, and
pent! Re - pent, they shout in warn - ing bold, and
men!" "A - men!" we shout in glo - rious praise, and
Re - joice! Re - joice! Re - joice! Re - joice!
Re - pent! Re - pent! Re - pent! Re - pent!
A - men! A - men! A - men! A - men!
come and take on sec - ond birth. Come join with ours your
with all strength to glo - ry hold. Yes, this grand mes - sage
with all grat - i - tude we raise. Let sing all of the
Re-joice! Re-joice! Re - joice! Re - joice!
Re-pent! Re-pent! Re - pent! Re - pent!
A - men! A - men! A - men! A - men!
hap - py voice. Re - joice! Re - joice! Re - joice!
He has sent: Re - pent! Re - pent! Re - pent!
hosts of men, "A - men! A - men! A - men!"

Psalms 68:3
2 Nephi 4:30

65

General Hymns

Restoration Morning

Kevin G. Pace

Kevin G. Pace

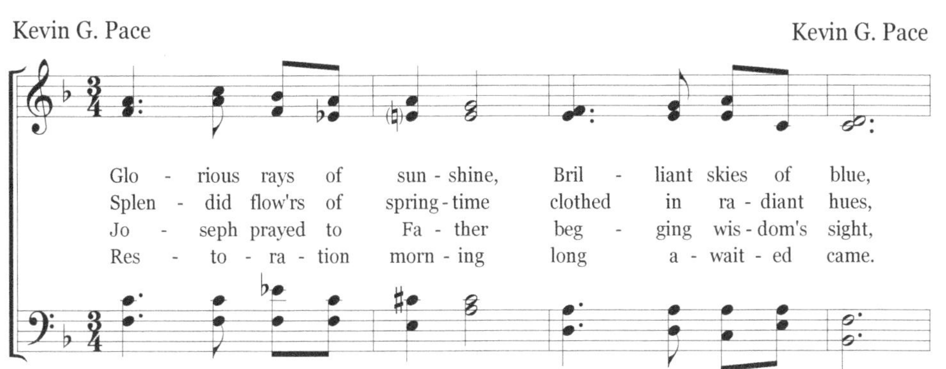

Glo - rious rays of sun - shine, Bril - liant skies of blue,
Splen - did flow'rs of spring - time clothed in ra - diant hues,
Jo - seph prayed to Fa - ther beg - ging wis - dom's sight,
Res - to - ra - tion morn - ing long a - wait - ed came.

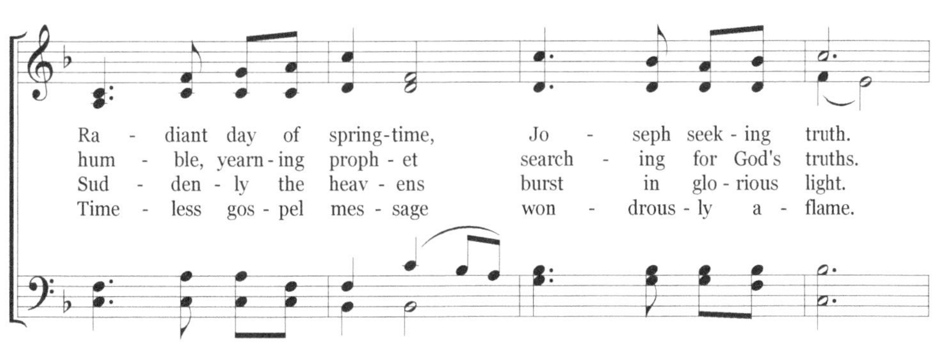

Ra - diant day of spring - time, Jo - seph seek - ing truth.
hum - ble, yearn - ing proph - et search - ing for God's truths.
Sud - den - ly the heav - ens burst in glo - rious light.
Time - less gos - pel mes - sage won - drous - ly a - flame.

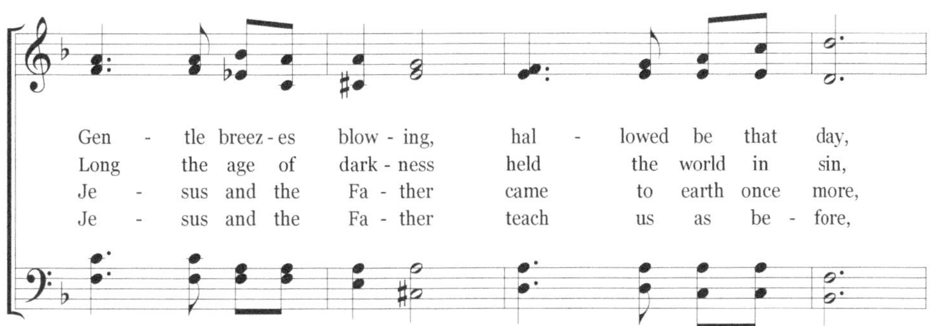

Gen - tle breez - es blow - ing, hal - lowed be that day,
Long the age of dark - ness held the world in sin,
Je - sus and the Fa - ther came to earth once more,
Je - sus and the Fa - ther teach us as be - fore,

Jo - seph sought the Fath - er, kneel - ing there to pray.
Now the heav'ns would o - pen, God to speak a - gain.
Speak - ing to a proph - et, bring - ing truths as - sured.
With the ho - ly an - gels, all has been re - stored.
Jo - seph sought the Fath - er, kneel - ing there to pray.
Now the heav'ns would o - pen, God to speak a - gain.
Speak - ing to a proph - et, bring - ing truths as - sured.
With the ho - ly an - gels, all has been re - stored.

Joseph Smith History 1:17-20
John 14:27

66

General Hymns

Share Goodness

Michael Young

Rick Graham

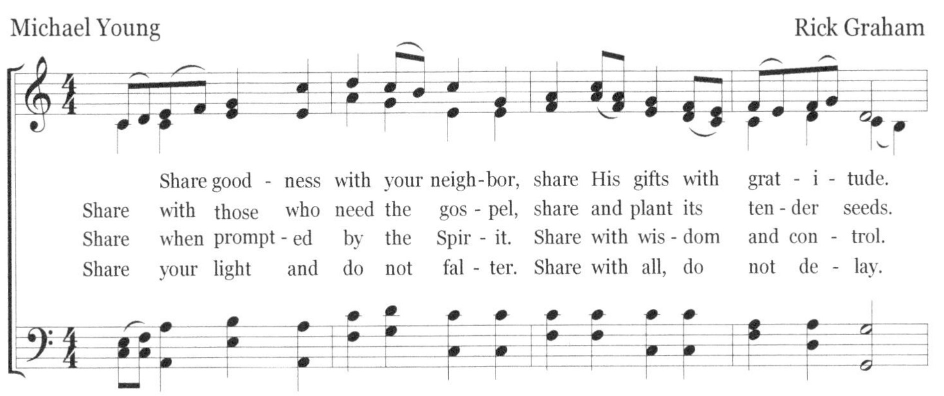
Share good - ness with your neigh-bor, share His gifts with grat - i - tude.
Share with those who need the gos - pel, share and plant its ten - der seeds.
Share when prompt - ed by the Spir - it. Share with wis - dom and con - trol.
Share your light and do not fal - ter. Share with all, do not de - lay.

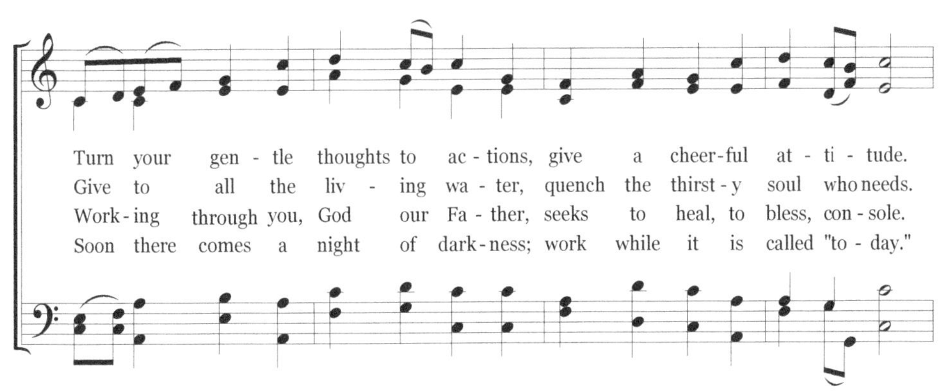
Turn your gen - tle thoughts to ac - tions, give a cheer-ful at - ti - tude.
Give to all the liv - ing wa - ter, quench the thirst - y soul who needs.
Work - ing through you, God our Fa - ther, seeks to heal, to bless, con - sole.
Soon there comes a night of dark - ness; work while it is called "to - day."

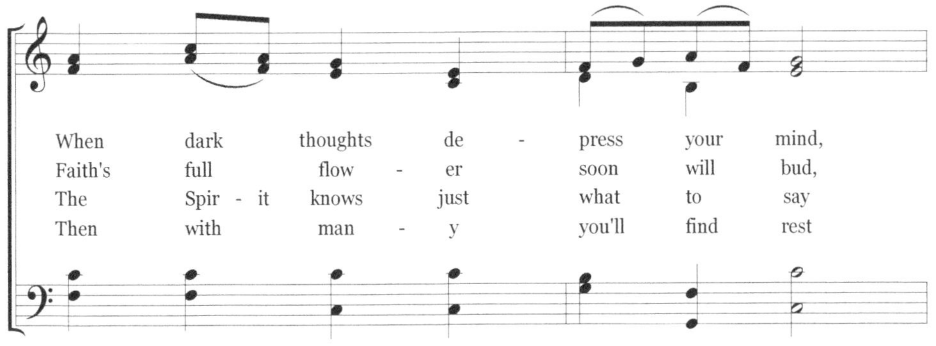
When dark thoughts de - press your mind,
Faith's full flow - er soon will bud,
The Spir - it knows just what to say
Then with man - y you'll find rest

drive them out with ser - vice kind. Share God's good - ness
as these drops be - come a flood! Share with those who
to each one in His own way. Share when prompt - ed
in our Fa - ther's king - dom blessed. Share your light and

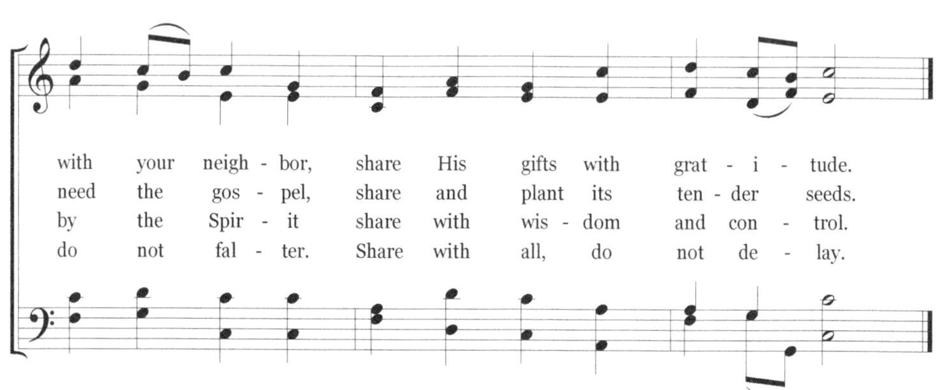
with your neigh - bor, share His gifts with grat - i - tude.
need the gos - pel, share and plant its ten - der seeds.
by the Spir - it share with wis - dom and con - trol.
do not fal - ter. Share with all, do not de - lay.

Mosiah 2:17
Mosiah 4:15

67 Sing All Praise to God the Father

General Hymns

Dianne Killburn

Jana McGettigan

Sing all praise to God the Fa-ther and His Son, our ris-en Lord. Let our
We as-sem-ble as a wit-ness of our faith in Je-sus Christ. We re-
May our hearts and hands be ho-ly, as the sac-ra-ment is blessed. May our
voic-es join in cho-rus and cre-ate a heav'n-ly chord.
mem-ber that He suf-fered, and up-on the cross He died. Hal-le-
true de-light be liv-ing in the way of righ-teous-ness.
lu-iah, hal-le-lu-jah, per fect is Thy plan of love. Hal-le-
lu-jah, Hal-le-lu-jah. May we dwell with Thee a-bove.
rit.

Alma 36:22
2 Nephi 31:13

68 Stick of Joseph, Stick of Judah

General Hymns

Michael D. Young
Kevin G. Pace
In E - den, then in Ca - naan's land, In Is - ra - el was heard The
First in a sta - ble as a child, On shores of Gal - i - lee, Some
In wil - der - ness and on the sea, Then in the Prom - ised Land. Both
The Stick of Ju - dah is one voice, The Stick of Jo - seph u - nites Its
voice of God, both still and grand, Proph - ets wrote His ho - ly word. The
heard Christ's words, pure, un - de - filed, Man - y wrote what they did see. The
Ne - phi and his seed were free, And did God's grace un - der - stand. The
wit - ness - es, and gives us choice, Of heed - ing both of these two lights. Two
Stick of Ju - dah lent its voice, It wit - nessed of the Christ to come, And
Stick of Ju - dah grew a - gain, It wit - nessed of the Christ who came. How
Stick of Jo - seph then sprang up, It wit - nessed of the Christ as well, Of
wit - ness - es of Christ who lives, Who came and yet will come a - gain, Un -
mak - ing all who read re - joice, It was the part, but not the sum.
once our Sav - ior dwelt with men, And cleansed man - kind of sin and blame.
Him who drained the bit - ter cup, Re - deem - ing them from death and hell.
til that time, His words He gives, Yet none may know the ho - ur when.

Ezekiel 37:16-19

69 Thanksgiving

General Hymns

Rick Graham | Rick Graham

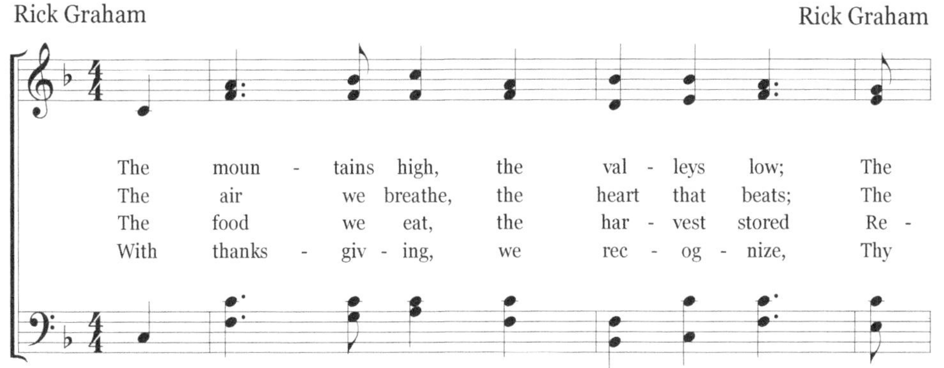
The moun - tains high, the val - leys low; The
The air we breathe, the heart that beats; The
The food we eat, the har - vest stored Re -
With thanks - giv - ing, we rec - og - nize, Thy

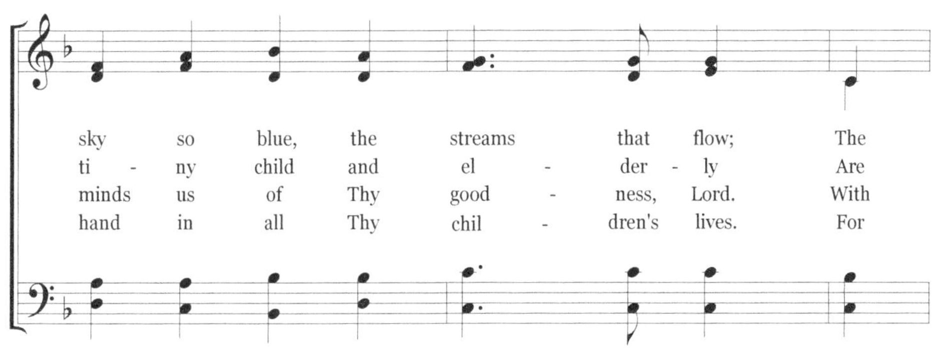
sky so blue, the streams that flow; The
ti - ny child and el - der - ly Are
minds us of Thy good - ness, Lord. With
hand in all Thy chil - dren's lives. For

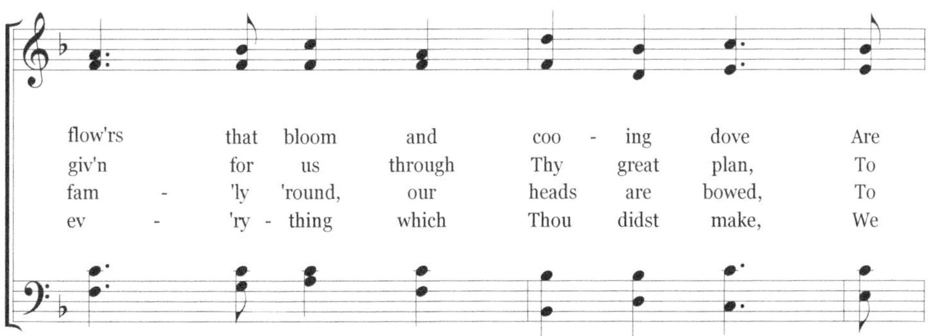
flow'rs that bloom and coo - ing dove Are
giv'n for us through Thy great plan, To
fam - 'ly 'round, our heads are bowed, To
ev - 'ry - thing which Thou didst make, We

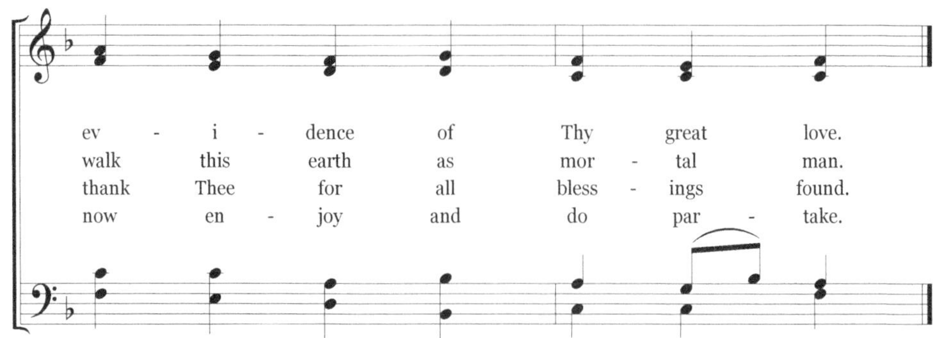
ev - i - dence of Thy great love.
walk this earth as mor - tal man.
thank Thee for all bless - ings found.
now en - joy and do par - take.

Psalms 26:7
Psalms 100:4

The Book of Mormon

Mark R. Fotheringham

Kevin G. Pace

Sa - cred words en - grav - en in gold ___ in Cum - or - ah lay.
Jo - seph seek - ing to know ___ his state ap - proached the throne of grace.
Stick of Ju - dah, stick ___ of Jo - seph, in thy hand are one.
Prop - hets' voic - es ___ from the past who once ___ had seen our day. From the
Clothed in glo - ry an an - gel of God ap - peared be - fore his face. He was
Tes - ti - fy - ing that God is our Lord the Fa - ther's bless - ed Son. With a
dust they would whis - per to ___ the heart, Truth un - tar - nished to im - part,
called by the an - gel to a great work. He ___ would trans - late the sa - cred book,
prom - ise to all who stud - y and pray, You can know of its truth to - day.
Wait - ing there for an age to ___ pass, gath - ered by prop - hets of old.
Free - ing voic - es ___ from the dust, - Scrip - ture to show us the way.
Book of Mor - mon, Ho - ly ___ Word, sent ___ to gath - er His fold.

Mormon 1:1
Articles of Faith 1:8

71 The Disciple's Prayer

General Hymns

Daniel R. Mercer

Jonah D. Hadlock

Fa - ther in Heav - en, Oh, we love Thee dear - ly; bless us this day that
Guide us with the voice of Thy Spir - it, cleanse our hearts that
As we for - give wilt Thou for - give our fail - lings, grant us strength to
we may live sin - cere - ly. Make us a means to
we may hear it. Let us not make
mag - ni - fy our cal - lings? Help us, through faith, give
spread Thy truth a - broad, that we may share the glo - rious word of God.
an - y de - lay, but, with all haste, go lis - ten and o - bey.
ser - vice from our hearts that we, in our-selves, a bet - ter life may start.

John 13:35

The Father, Son, and Holy Ghost

Bradley Hampton

Bradley Hampton

Our Fa - ther, God and Ho - ly King, We
Our Fa - ther's Son; He suf - fered all To
The Spir - it is the Ho - ly Ghost. He
We give great thanks for ev - 'ry - thing That

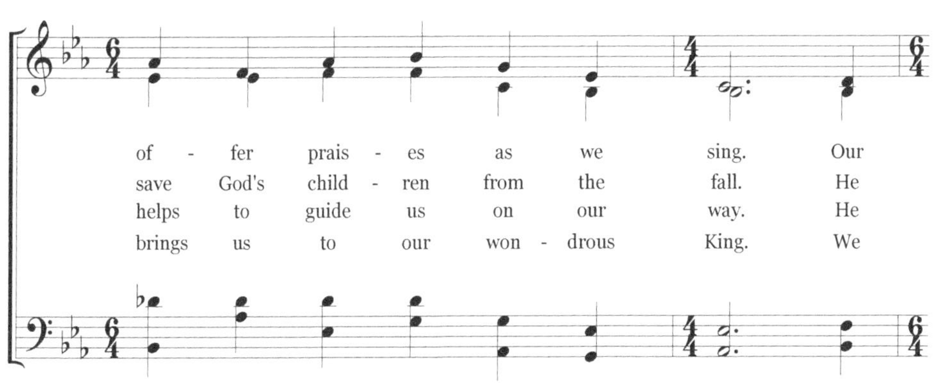
of - fer prais - es as we sing. Our
save God's child - ren from the fall. He
helps to guide us on our way. He
brings us to our won - drous King. We

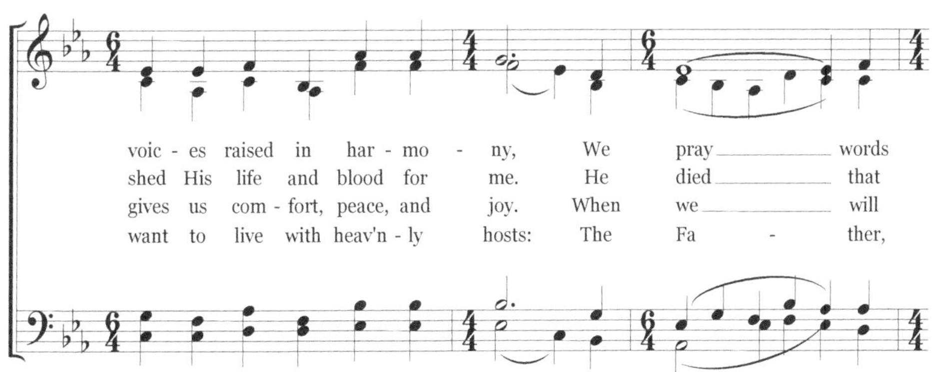
voic - es raised in har - mo - ny, We pray words
shed His life and blood for me. He died that
gives us com - fort, peace, and joy. When we will
want to live with heav'n - ly hosts: The Fa - ther,

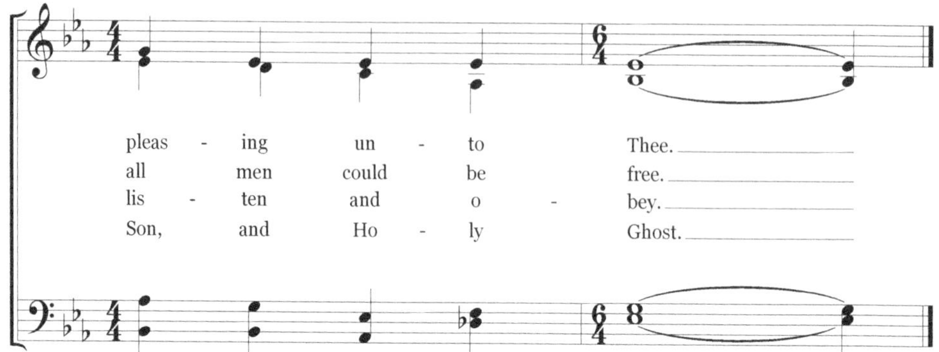
pleas - ing un - to Thee.
all men could be free.
lis - ten and o - bey.
Son, and Ho - ly Ghost.

Articles of Faith 1:1

73 The Gospel of Our Lord

General Hymns

Christian S. Draper — Christian S. Draper

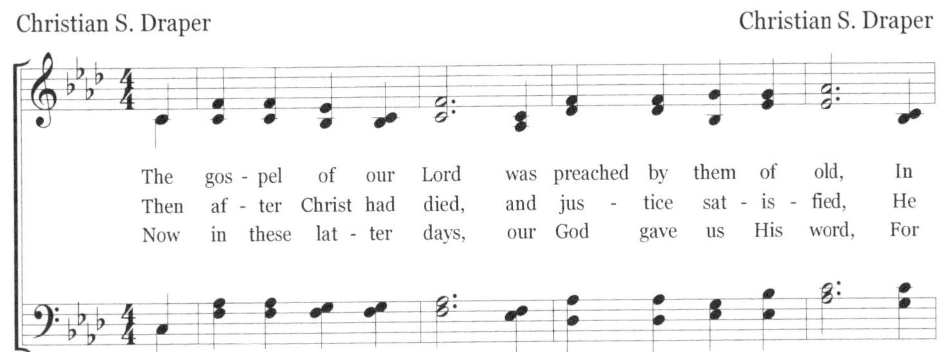
The gos - pel of our Lord was preached by them of old, In
Then af - ter Christ had died, and jus - tice sat - is - fied, He
Now in these lat - ter days, our God gave us His word, For

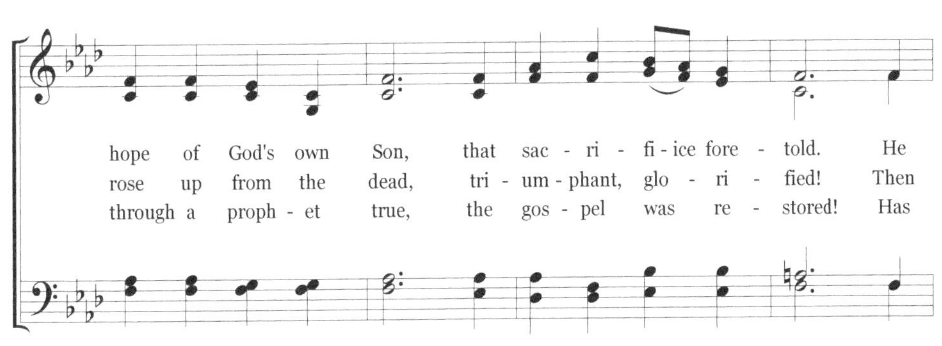
hope of God's own Son, that sac - ri - fi - ice fore - told. He
rose up from the dead, tri - um - phant, glo - ri - fied! Then
through a proph - et true, the gos - pel was re - stored! Has

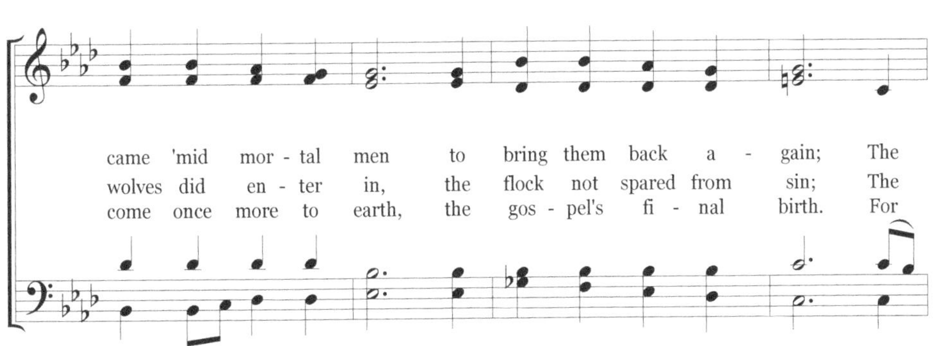
came 'mid mor - tal men to bring them back a - gain; The
wolves did en - ter in, the flock not spared from sin; The
come once more to earth, the gos - pel's fi - nal birth. For

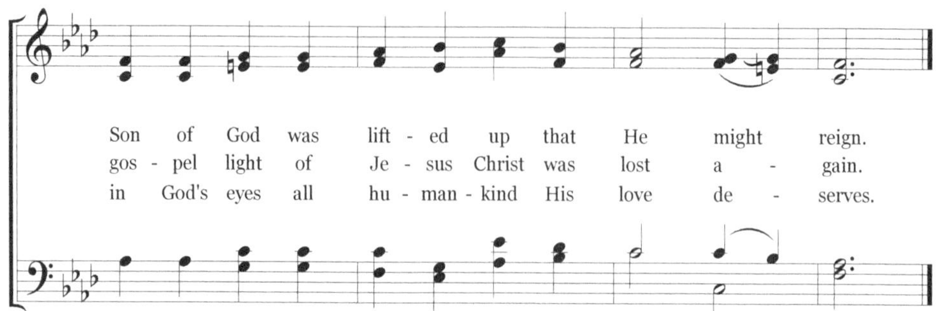
Son of God was lift - ed up that He might reign.
gos - pel light of Je - sus Christ was lost a - gain.
in God's eyes all hu - man - kind His love de - serves.

JST, John 1:4
Doctrine and Covenants 39:5

The One Sure Light

Gary Croxall — Kathleen Holyoak

In

all my trials the Lord at - tends, I nev - er walk a - lone. He
takes my hand and gent - ly leads a - long life's thorn - y way; He
I grow faint, Christ bears me up and lifts my heav - y load. He

stands be - side me in the night; He points the way back home. The
marks the path that I should walk and teach - es me to pray. The
shel - ters me from rain and wind up - on__ the storm - y road. He

Lord is might - y and shall save each soul who trusts in Him. The
Sav - ior, Cap - tain of my soul, di - rects and leads a - right. The
strength-ens me as I press on, un - til the vic - t'ry's won. The

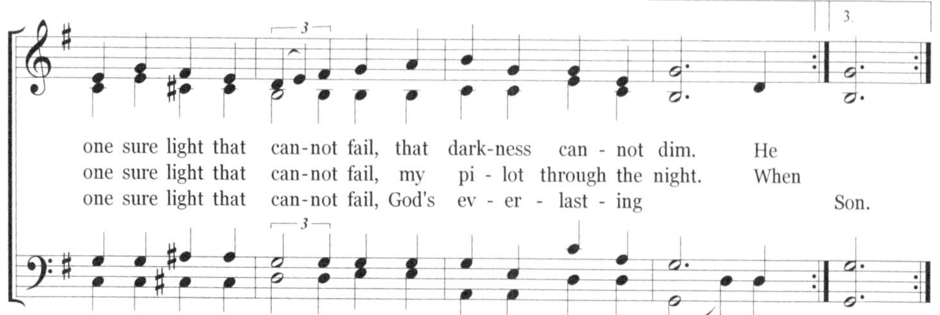
3.
one sure light that can-not fail, that dark-ness can - not dim. He
one sure light that can-not fail, my pi - lot through the night. When
one sure light that can-not fail, God's ev - er - last - ing Son.

Mosiah 16:9
Psalms 36:9

75 The Promised Day Must Soon Break Forth

General Hymns

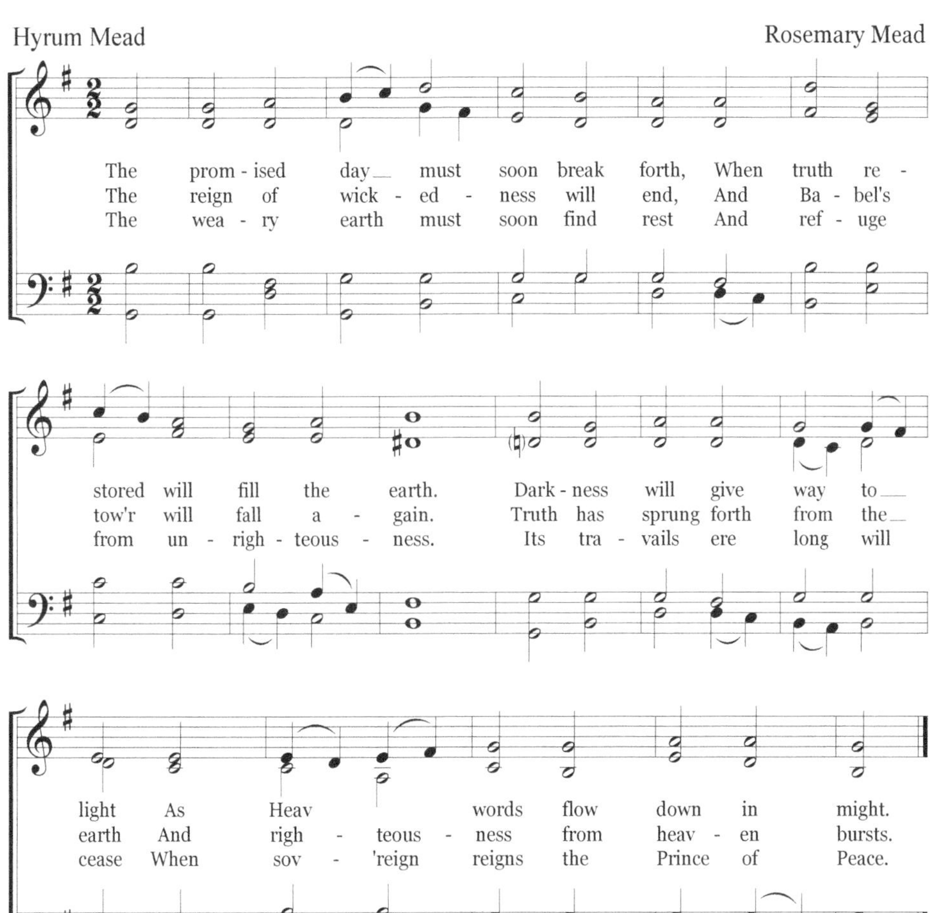
Hyrum Mead
Rosemary Mead
The prom - ised day must soon break forth, When truth re -
The reign of wick - ed - ness will end, And Ba - bel's
The wea - ry earth must soon find rest And ref - uge
stored will fill the earth. Dark - ness will give way to
tow'r will fall a - gain. Truth has sprung forth from the
from un - righ - teous - ness. Its tra - vails ere long will
light As Heav words flow down in might.
earth And righ - teous - ness from heav - en bursts.
cease When sov - 'reign reigns the Prince of Peace.

Doctrine and Covenants 128:19

76 There Is No Place So Far Away

Michael D. Young
Chad Staten
There is no place so far a - way, Be - yond the Sav - ior's reach. There
There is no place so cold and dark His warmth can - not break through. His
There is no hour so late that He would slum - ber and not hear The
There is no shame or stain so dire His life can - not a - tone. The
There is no pain or bit - ter loss Christ's blood can - not e - rase. No
is no wall or for - tress grey His vir - tue can - not breach. What
sac - ri - fice has left its mark that proves His love is true. For
hum - ble pray'r, the fer - vent plea, for ev - 'ry - one is dear. He
of - fer - ing He does re - quire: His will to do a - lone. He
mat - ter what our mor - tal cross, He brings peace in its place. He
glad - ness lights the Shep - herd's eye with each re - turn - ing sheep! In
what love must He then pos - sess to bleed from ev - 'ry pore? To
un - der - stands what we must face: temp - ta - tion, weak - ness, sin. And
of - fers us a way to think on what His love has wrought, With
takes our shat - tered piec - es lost, re - stores us glo - rious, whole, For
Him our hope of res - cue lies when we His pre - cepts keep.
un - der - go such great dur - ess, our spir - its to re - store?
brings through His a - bun - dant grace our vic - tor - y with - in.
sym - bols of His sac - ri - fice through which He us has bought.
He a - lone knows well the cost of ev - 'ry pre - cious soul!

Romans 8:35-39

77 The Restoration

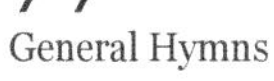

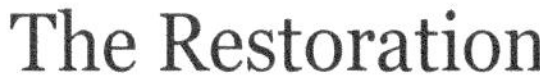

General Hymns

Gary Croxall

Kathleen Holyoak

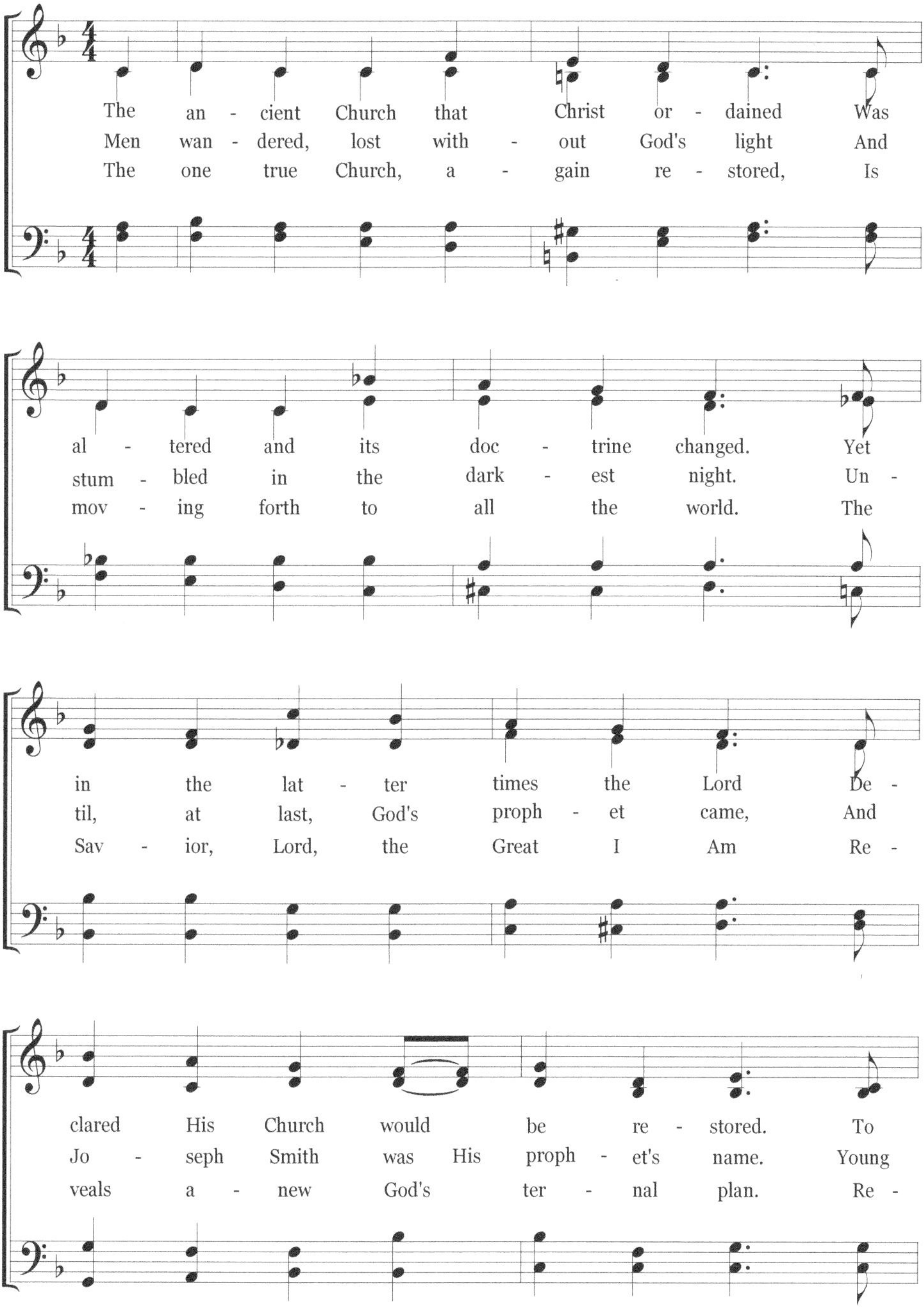

The ancient Church that Christ ordained Was
Men wandered, lost without God's light And
The one true Church, again restored, Is
altered and its doctrine changed. Yet
stumbled in the darkest night. Un-
moving forth to all the world. The
in the latter times the Lord De-
til, at last, God's prophet came, And
Savior, Lord, the Great I Am Re-
clared His Church would be restored. To
Joseph Smith was His prophet's name. Young
veals anew God's ternal plan. Re-

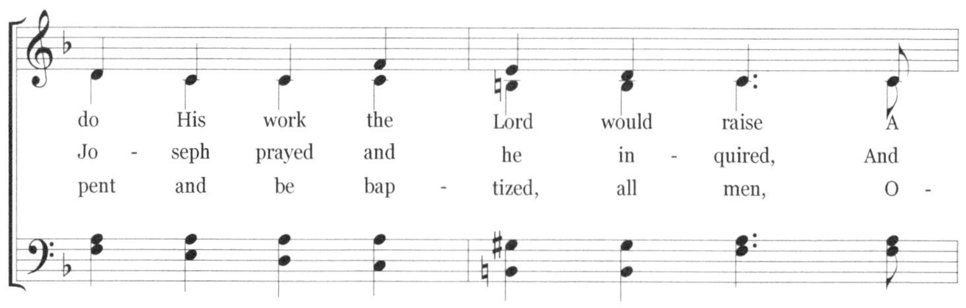
do His work the Lord would raise A
Jo - seph prayed and he in - quired, And
pent and be bap - tized, all men, O -

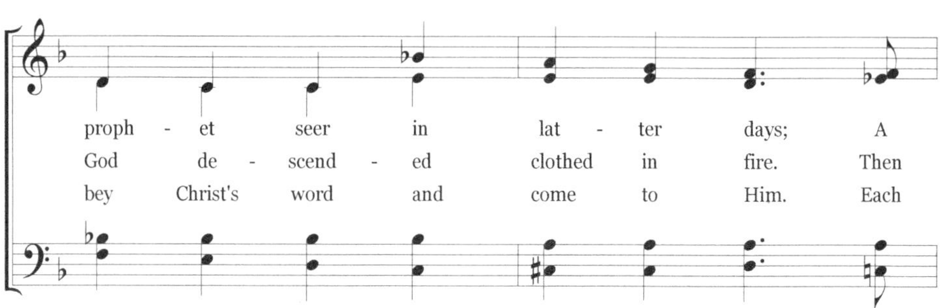
proph - et seer in lat - ter days; A
God de - scend - ed clothed in fire. Then
bey Christ's word and come to Him. Each

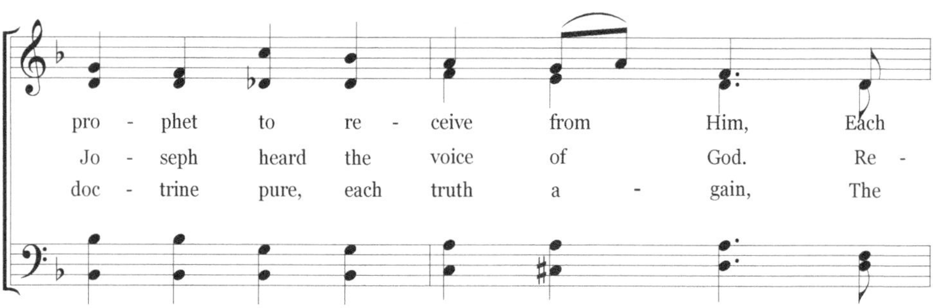
pro - phet to re - ceive from Him, Each
Jo - seph heard the voice of God. Re -
doc - trine pure, each truth a - gain, The

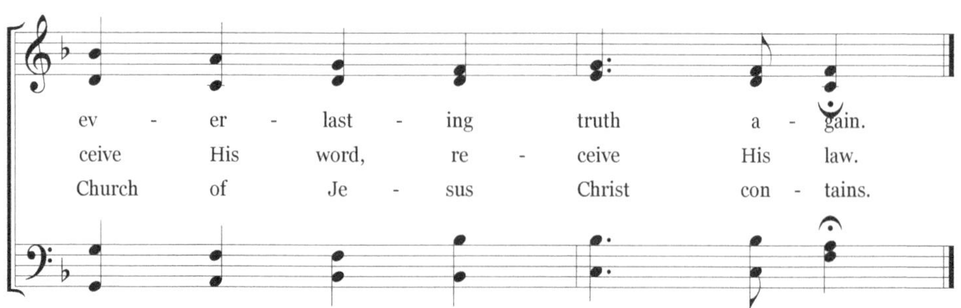
ev - er - last - ing truth a - gain.
ceive His word, re - ceive His law.
Church of Je - sus Christ con - tains.

Mormon 9:36
Doctrine and Covenants 27:6

The Sabbath Is a Sweet Delight

General Hymns

Michael D. Young

Daniel Kerr

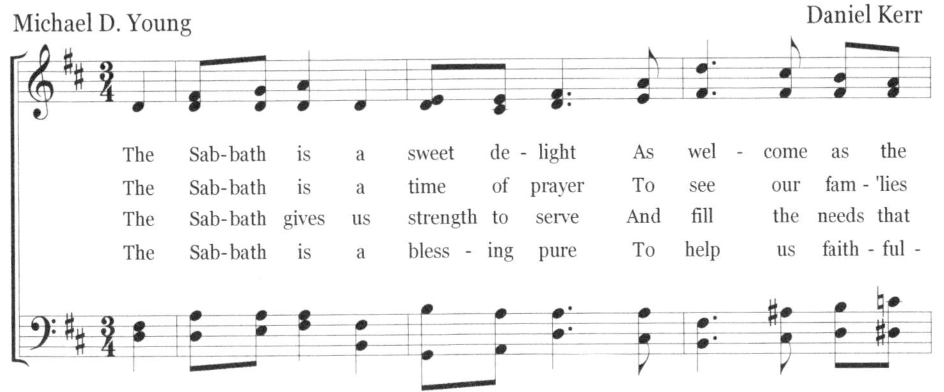

The Sab-bath is a sweet de - light As wel - come as the
The Sab-bath is a time of prayer To see our fam - 'lies
The Sab-bath gives us strength to serve And fill the needs that
The Sab-bath is a bless - ing pure To help us faith - ful -

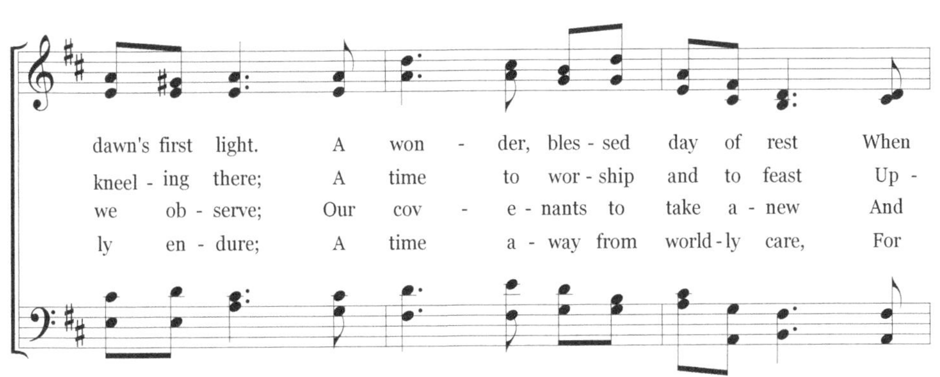

dawn's first light. A won - der, bles - sed day of rest When
kneel - ing there; A time to wor - ship and to feast Up -
we ob - serve; Our cov - e - nants to take a - new And
ly en - dure; A time a - way from world - ly care, For

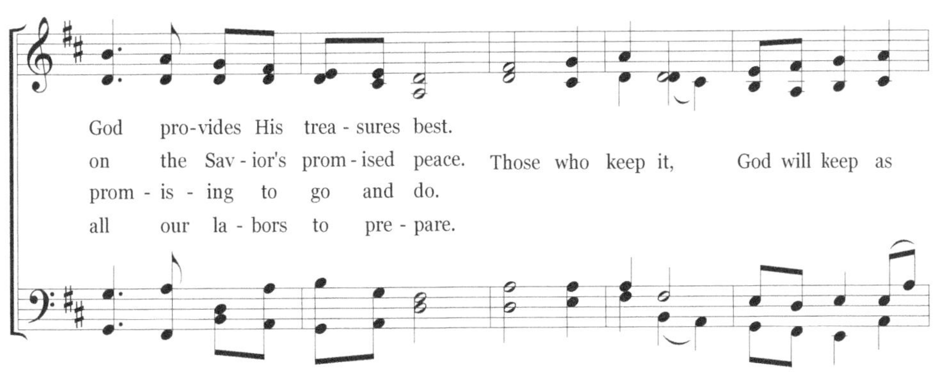

God pro-vides His trea - sures best.
on the Sav - ior's prom - ised peace. Those who keep it, God will keep as
prom - is - ing to go and do.
all our la - bors to pre - pare.

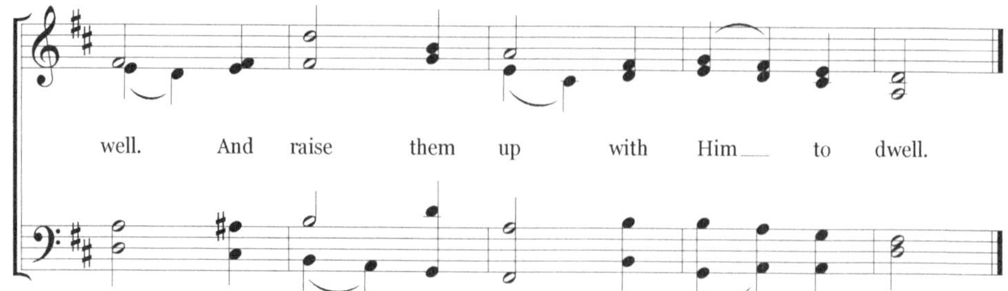
well. And raise them up with Him to dwell.

Isaiah 58:13-14

The Song of Redeeming Love

General Hymns

Max G. Walters

Max G. Walters

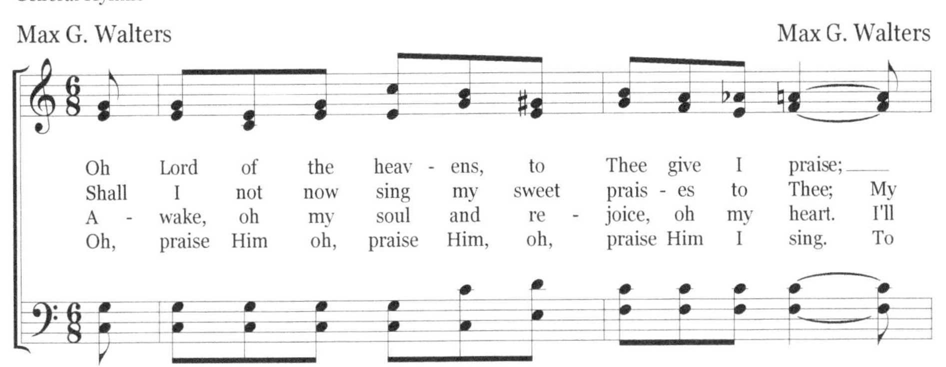
Oh Lord of the heav - ens, to Thee give I praise;
Shall I not now sing my sweet prais - es to Thee; My
A - wake, oh my soul and re - joice, oh my heart. I'll
Oh, praise Him oh, praise Him, oh, praise Him I sing. To

Praise and re - joic - ing are now my new ways. I'll
life from here on shall be pleas - ing, you'll see. My
love Thee and serve Thee and now do my part. Thy
Thee, my dear Sav - ior, will-ing heart do I bring. I re -

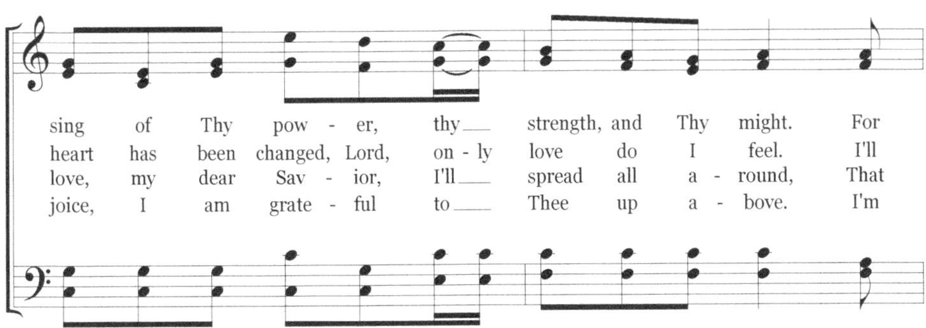
sing of Thy pow - er, thy strength, and Thy might. For
heart has been changed, Lord, on - ly love do I feel. I'll
love, my dear Sav - ior, I'll spread all a - round, That
joice, I am grate - ful to Thee up a - bove. I'm

time ev - er - more I will do what is right.
praise Thee for - ev - er, my heart thou didst heal.
on - ly pure love 'mongst Thy chil - dren is found.
ran - somed, I'm clean. I'm re - deemed by Thy love.
Oh Sav - ior Re - deem - er, of Thee will I boast.
God of the heav - ens, Lord of the Host. Praise to my Sav -
- high up a - bove I'm ran-somed, I'm clean. I'm re-deemed by Thy love.

Alma 5:26

80 Thunder Must Roar

General Hymns

Norma Boyd | Norma Boyd

In times of great tri - al when look-ing a - round, You see oth - er
We are as the flow - ers, our tri - als like rain. Though hard to en -
peo - ple. Their bles - sings a - bound; The sin - ful, the wick - ed with
dure, we need sor - row and pain. For flow - ers love sun - shine and
nar - y a care. That God should bless them so, does - n't seem fair. But
grow t'ward the sky, But with - out rain - drops they'd with - er and die. So
in - to each life the thun - der must sure - ly roar, And

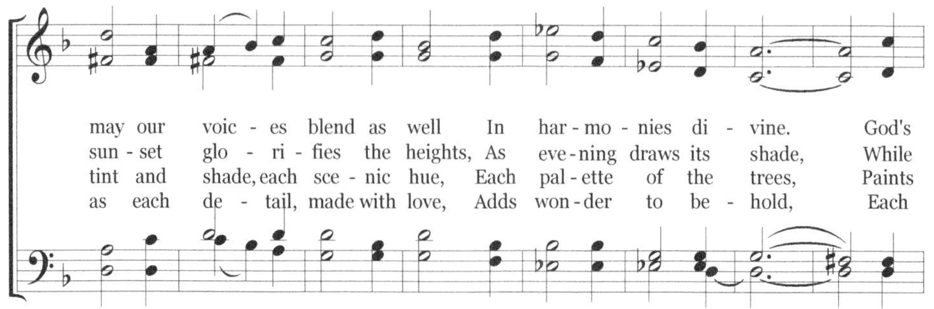
may our voic - es blend as well In har - mo - nies di - vine. God's
sun - set glo - ri - fies the heights, As eve - ning draws its shade, While
tint and shade, each sce - nic hue, Each pal - ette of the trees, Paints
as each de - tail, made with love, Adds won - der to be - hold, Each

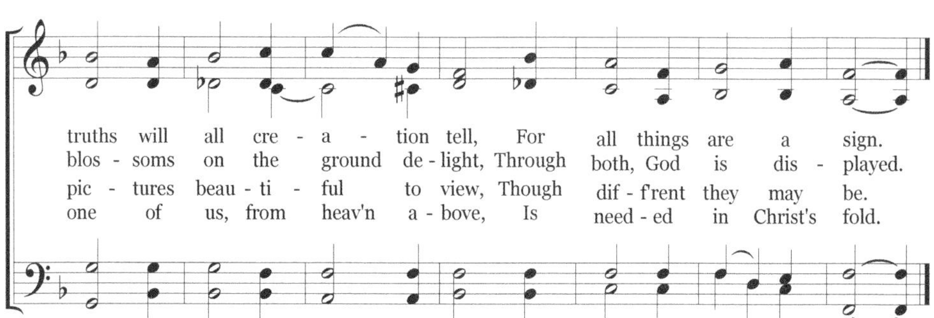
truths will all cre - a - tion tell, For all things are a sign.
blos - soms on the ground de - light, Through both, God is dis - played.
pic - tures beau - ti - ful to view, Though dif - f'rent they may be.
one of us, from heav'n a - bove, Is need - ed in Christ's fold.

Moses 7:18

81 Two Birds That Sing from Branches High

Angie Mae Killian and Michael D. Young

Kevin G. Pace

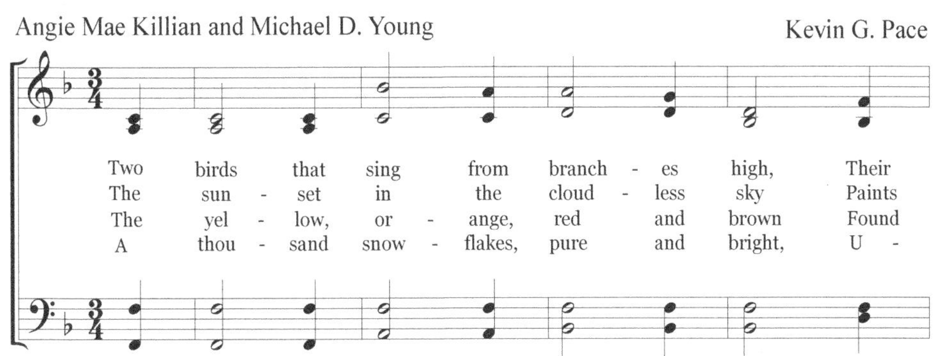
Two birds that sing from branch - es high, Their
The sun - set in the cloud - less sky Paints
The yel - low, or - ange, red and brown Found
A thou - sand snow - flakes, pure and bright, U -

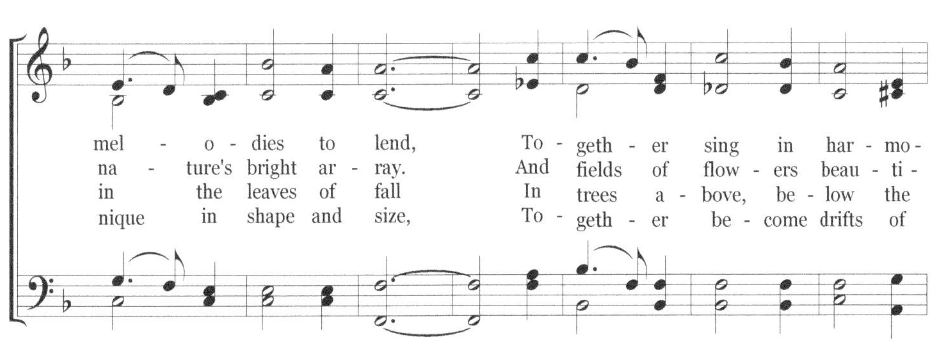
mel - o - dies to lend, To - geth - er sing in har - mo -
na - ture's bright ar - ray. And fields of flow - ers beau - ti -
in the leaves of fall In trees a - bove, be - low the
nique in shape and size, To - geth - er be - come drifts of

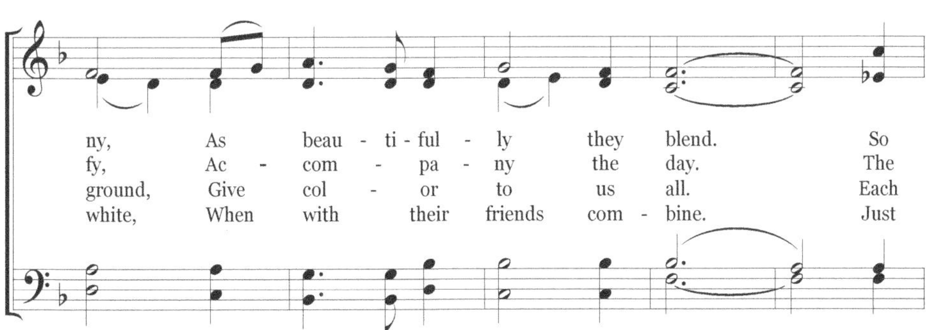
ny, As beau - ti - ful - ly they blend. So
fy, Ac - com - pa - ny the day. The
ground, Give col - or to us all. Each
white, When with their friends com - bine. Just

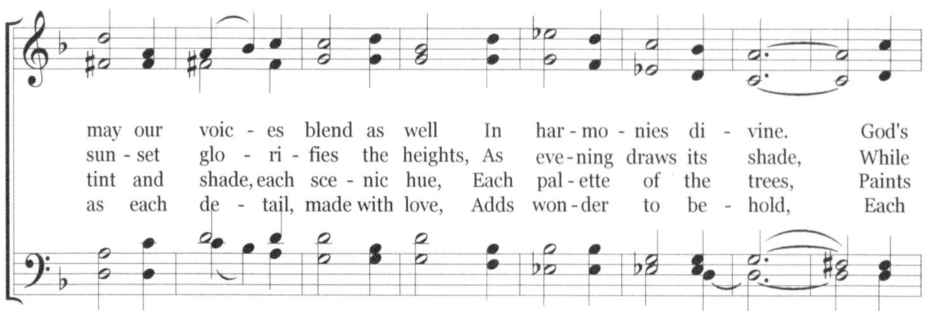

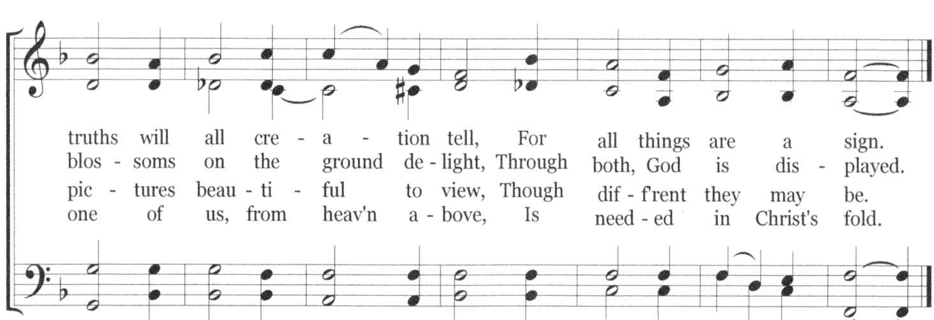

Moses 7:18

Upon Wings of Prayer

Sherry Summers

Kathleen Holyoak

Re - lease ev - 'ry care up - on wings of prayer,
A - wak - en the flame with - in me a - gain.
Dis - ci - ple and friend, a ves - sel for Him,
The Lord is my rock; in Him will I trust,
yield - ing to Fa - ther sub - lime. As
Ban - ish the wor - ry and care. A
I'll seek the lambs of His fold.
es - sence of wis - dom and truth. In
shad - ows dis - pel ten-der sor - rows de - part.
pri - sm of tears re - flec - ting His Son,
bear up the faint for His heal - ing em - brace.
faith I re - solve to live as He taught.

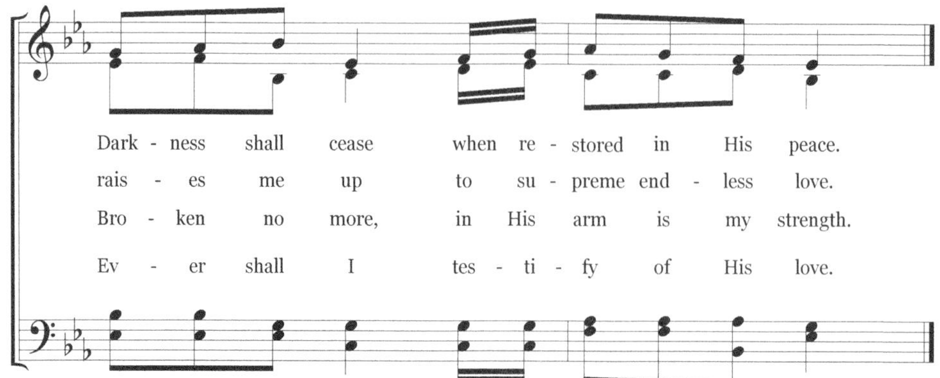
Dark - ness shall cease when re - stored in His peace.
rais - es me up to su - preme end - less love.
Bro - ken no more, in His arm is my strength.
Ev - er shall I tes - ti - fy of His love.

Doctrine and Covenants 29:2
Doctrine and Covenants 10:5

83

General Hymns

We Add Our Voice

Michael D. Young

Norma Boyd

To what the an - cient proph-ets said, we glad - ly raise our voice. We're
To what the mod - ern proph-ets speak, we glad - ly do sus - tain. For
act - ing on the words we've read and stand - ing by our choice. To
they in - vig - o - rate the weak and make the gos - pel plain. To
what the lat - ter proph-ets spoke, we glad - ly shout, "A - men!" In
what our pres - ent proph-ets speak, we glad - ly shout, "A - men!" The
them the Res - to - ra - tion woke, Christ's Church re - stored a - gain.
gos - pel mes - sage, clear and sweet is on the earth a - gain.

Amos 3:7

84 What Greater Peace?

General Hymns

Michael D. Young

Michael D. Young

What great-er peace can mor - tals know? What great-er gifts does
What great-er joy can one pos - sess? What great-er fount of
What great-er light can one per - ceive? What great-er rea - son
What great-er love can one heart feel? What great-er wit - ness
God be - stow? Than in His ho - ly house of prayer.
ho - li - ness? Than in the hal - lowed walls sub - lime
to be - lieve? Than in the pal - ace of our King,
that God's real? Than kneel-ing at His throne and feet,
For He, Him - self, is dwell - ing there.
Of tem - ples in this lat - ter time.
Where ho - ly an - gels walk and sing.
Where hap - pi - ness is whole, com - plete.

John 14:27
2 Nephi 12:2-3

85 When Godly Sorrow Moves the Soul

General Hymns

David Macfarlane

Nathan Howe

When God - ly sor - row moves the soul To lay on
A voice of mild - ness pricks the heart When law and
He paid our debts and felt our pain, From oth - ers'
Our bur - dens lift - ed: oh what peace! And to at -
The voic - es of these lat - ter days En - tice the
Christ a debt of pride, The arms of love are reach - ing
con - science are be - trayed; To make a - mends we do our
choic - es and our own, That we might be made whole a -
tain Thy ho - ly place, May we for - give our fel - low
no - ble and the great; Yet ev - 'ry bles - sing comes to
out, Where - in the wound - ed heart may hide.
part, Yet must re - ly on Je - sus's aid.
gain And know His pres - ence as our home.
man As Thou hast shown us liv - ing grace.
those who walk the path, though steep and strait.

2 Corinthians 7:9-11

86 When the Savior Comes Again

General Hymns

Andrew Moore
Andrew Moore
Zi - on, pre-pare for the time and sea - son now at hand. The
Stal - wart and faith - ful, the Saints shall stand in ho - ly plac - es
Fear not the fu - ture, when hold - ing to the rod of i - ron.
Great is the day when the Lord re - turns in pow'r and glo - ry,
world a - waits His com - ing in these, the lat - ter days.
Guard - ing ev - 'ry vir - tue, de - fend - ing truth and right.
Ev - er straight and nar - row, the path of righ - teous - ness,
Heav'n - ly hosts at - tend - ing, in tri - umph, praise His name.
Proph - ets have spo - ken, their proph - e - cies are now ful - fill - ing,
Gath - ered to - geth - er, they'll safe - ty find in stakes of Zi - on,
Leads to the pres - ence of He who then will reign su - preme, Pre -
Shouts of Ho - san - na, as choirs of an - gels sing with joy, For
Has - ten - ing the day when the Sav - ior comes a - gain.
Watch - ing for the day when the Sav - ior comes a - gain.
pare ye for the day when the Sav - ior comes a - gain.
this shall be the day when our Sav - ior comes a - gain.

Doctrine and Covenants 34:6
Doctrine and Covenants 88:99

87

Always Remember Him

Sacrament Hymns

Jeff Kocherhans
Jeff Kocherhans
unison
In a dark and lone - ly gar - den on an aw - ful
When I think of all He suf - fered just be - cause He
Two long nights, He lay in dark - ness. Death had con - quered,
Some - day He'll come down from heav - en. I will run to
cross of wood Je - sus res - cued me from dark - ness,
loves me so, My heart longs to serve Him al - ways
so it seemed. Then, what joy! As the third day dawned, He
His em - brace. With His wound - ed hands He'll bless
bought my free - dom with His blood. Al - le -
and be true to all I know.
rose with heal - ing in His wings.
wipe all tears that wet my face.
lu - ia! Al - le - lu - ia! I will al - ways re - mem - ber Him. A - le-

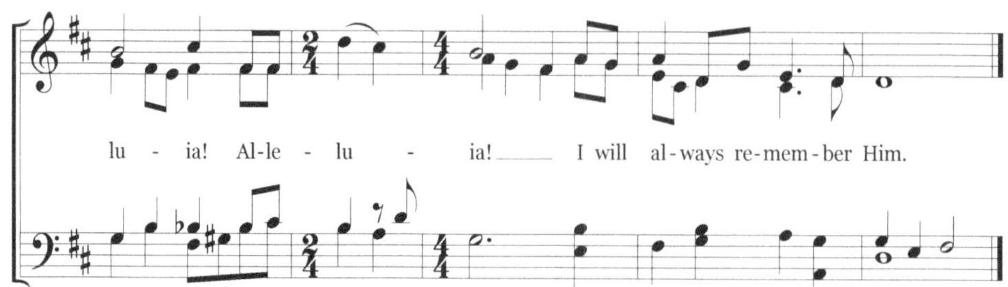
lu - ia! Al-le - lu - ia! I will al-ways re-mem-ber Him.

Moroni 4:3

88 As If from Thine Own Wounded Hand

Sacrament Hymns

Jeff Kocherhans

Jeff Kocherhans

As if from Thine own wound - ed hand We
Thy trem - bling in Geth - sem - a - ne, Thine
As friends to Thine own ta - ble, Lord, We
Oh Je - sus, nour - ish us to - day, Thou
take these sym - bols of Thy grace, Whose
a - gon - y up - on the cross Have
come in - vit - ed to par - take, And
bread of life and liv - ing spring, And
blood paid all our de - mand, Whose
drawn us by Thy love to Thee With
share the feast of Thy re - ward Bought
may we though the veil re - main, Feel
flesh was bro - ken in our place.
bro - ken hearts to view Thy loss.
by Thy suf - f'ring for our sake.
Thy em - brace, our lov - ing King!

Zechariah 13:6
Doctrine and Covenants 6:37

89 Bread of Life and Living Water

Sacrament Hymns

Orson Scott Card
Jana McGettigan
Bread of life and liv-ing wat-er, Pass-ing now from hand to hand, Will u-nite each son and daugh-ter In the path their Fa-ther planned.
As we take the sa-cred tok-en Of the Shep-herd who was slain, All our hearts are new-ly bro-ken For our part in Je-sus's pain. Look with
All our sins can be for-giv-en By the giv-er of the gift. Mas-ter of all earth and heav-en: He will span that hope-less rift.
love at one an-oth-er: None are strang-ers in this place. Ev-'ry sis-ter, ev-'ry broth-er has come home through Je-sus's grace.

John 6:51
Doctrine and Covenants 63:23

Heal Our Souls

David Featherstone — David Featherstone

Heal our souls with sweet for - giv - ing. Grant us fa - vor
Smile up - on our con - gre - ga - tion, While the sac - ra -
Gath - er in Thy Saints a - bout Thee, Ten - der bo - som
This Thy day of cel - e - bra - tion, Peace and rest un -
in Thy sight. Ban - ish thoughts of sin re - liv - ing,
ment we bless. Hum - bly now our rep - a - ra - tion
each to feel. Cra - dle faith till ne'er a doubt be
to our souls. Let our prayers of sup - pli - ca - tion
That we'll ev - er choose the right, That we'll ev - er choose the right.
As Thy ho - ly name con - fess, As Thy ho - ly name con - fess.
That Thy love for us is real, That Thy love for us is real.
Sa - cred be to make us whole, Sa - cred be to make us whole.

Malachi 4:2
2 Nephi 25:13

91 His Love Divine

Sacrament Hymns

Michael D. Young

Rick Graham

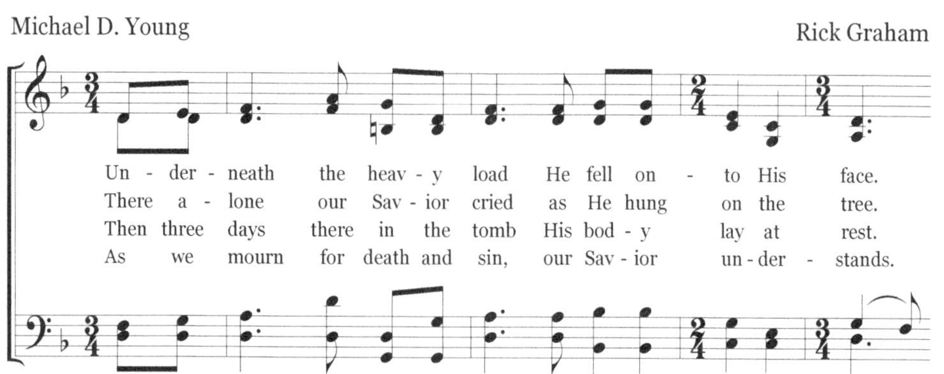
Un - der - neath the heav - y load He fell on - to His face.
There a - lone our Sav - ior cried as He hung on the tree.
Then three days there in the tomb His bod - y lay at rest.
As we mourn for death and sin, our Sav - ior un - der - stands.

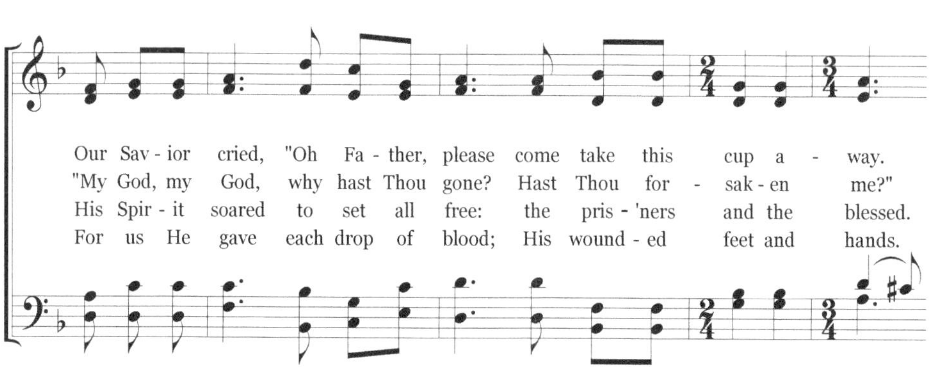
Our Sav - ior cried, "Oh Fa - ther, please come take this cup a - way.
"My God, my God, why hast Thou gone? Hast Thou for - sak - en me?"
His Spir - it soared to set all free: the pris - 'ners and the blessed.
For us He gave each drop of blood; His wound - ed feet and hands.

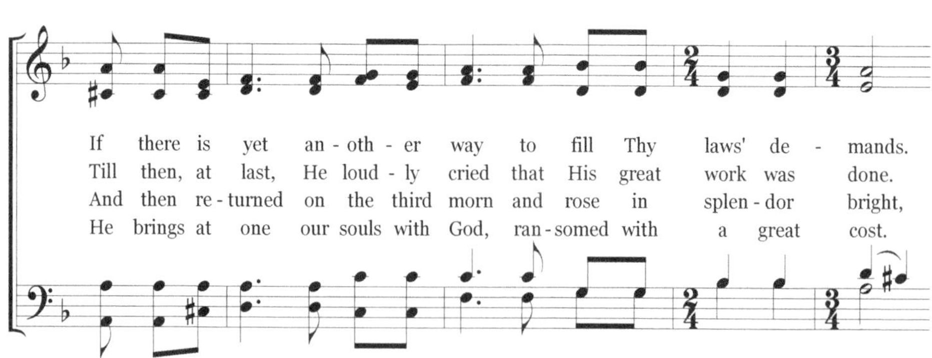
If there is yet an - oth - er way to fill Thy laws' de - mands.
Till then, at last, He loud - ly cried that His great work was done.
And then re - turned on the third morn and rose in splen - dor bright,
He brings at one our souls with God, ran - somed with a great cost.

But if not, then I will give My will in - to Thy hands."
Now His mor - tal life com - plete The fi - nal vic - t'ry won.
Per - fect - ly re - stored a - new and with an end - less light.
He paid through His love di - vine that we must not be lost.

Mark 14:32-36
Matthew 26: 36-42

92 I Did, Too

Sacrament Hymns

Michael D. Young — Norma Boyd

If you feel re - ject - ed, a - lone, If you feel you are on your
If you feel de - spised and op - pressed, False - ly judged, and in great dis - tress,
Christ's true mes-sage can see you through, For He says to us, "I did too."
Christ's true mes-sage can see you through, For He says to us, "I did too."
If you feel ne - glect-ed, ill used, Rid - i - culed, tor - ment - ed, a - bused,
If you feel for - sak - en, be-trayed, If you feel a - ban-doned, dis-mayed,
Christ's true mes-sage can see you through, For He says to us, "I did, too."
Christ's true mes-sage can see you through, For He says to us, "I did, too."

Doctrine and Covenants 122-7-9

93

In Gethsemane

Esther Megargel

Esther Megargel

It was for us the Sav - ior knelt in Geth - sem - a - ne. Our
It was for us He hung and died up - on Cal - va - ry. The
It is for Him we take the bread in our sac - ra - ment. And
It is for Him we sing our praise through e - ter - ni - ty. Our
sins and pains He truly felt in Geth - sem - a - ne. We
cru - el sol - diers pierced His side up on Cal - va - ry. And
wor - ship Him who is our Head in our sac - ra - ment. And
voic - es grate - ful - ly we raise, through e - ter - ni - ty. The
know not how He suf - fered there, how great the load He chose to bear, or
for our sins He paid the price. His great A - tone - ment will suf - fice. O
through this cup of wa - ter pure our mem - 'ry of Him is made sure, and
Lamb of God has made us free. He lives that we might ran - somed be. Our

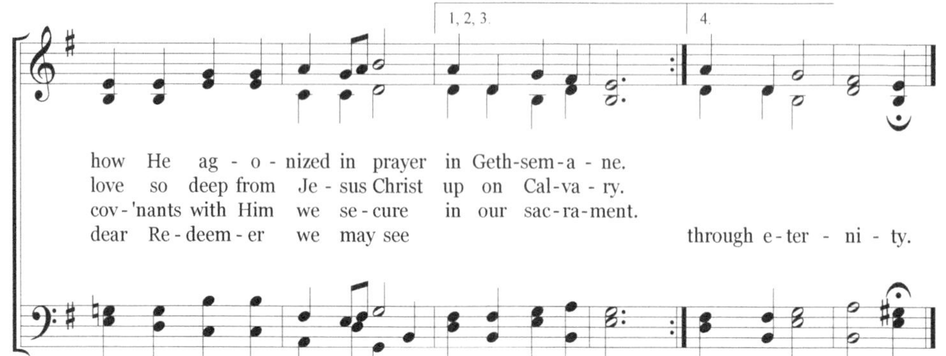
1, 2, 3.
4.
how He ag - o - nized in prayer in Geth-sem-a - ne.
love so deep from Je - sus Christ up on Cal-va - ry.
cov - 'nants with Him we se - cure in our sac - ra - ment.
dear Re - deem - er we may see through e - ter - ni - ty.

Matthew 26:36-43
Mark 14:32:41

94 In Token of Christ's Sacrifice

Gary Croxall Kathleen Holyoak

In to - ken of Christ's sac - ri - fice, we take the bread and wa - ter, Re -
Let each par - take whose hands are clean, whose love for God is cer - tain. Come
His blood and bod - y for us spent, Christ died a sin - less of - f'ring. Re -
new - ing sa - cred cov - e - nants un - to our Heav'n - ly Fa - ther. No
wor - ship His be - lov - ed - Son, who takes a - way sin's bur - den. Christ
mem - ber Him and think up - on His ag - o - ny and suf - f'ring. In
great - er love was ev - er shown than by our gen - tle Sav - ior; He
suf - fered in Geth - sem - a - ne; re - mem - ber His com - pas - sion. And
Him a - lone we have the hope of glo - ry and per - fec - tion. And

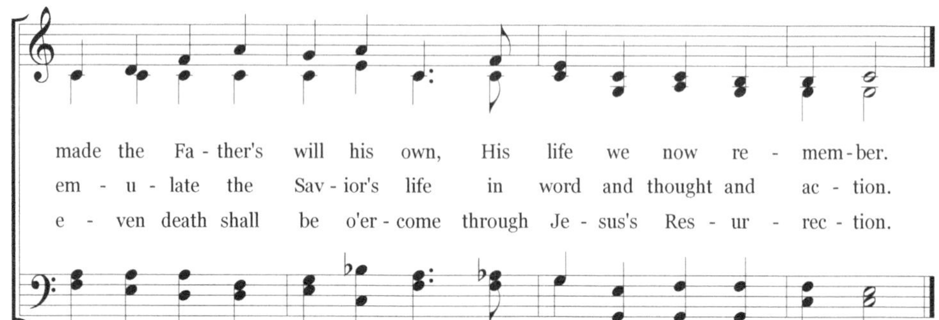
made the Fa - ther's will his own, His life we now re - mem - ber.
em - u - late the Sav - ior's life in word and thought and ac - tion.
e - ven death shall be o'er - come through Je - sus's Res - ur - rec - tion.

Luke 22:19
3 Nephi 18:6

95

Sacrament Hymns

O Savior Dear

Charles V. Anderson

Jared Bernotski

1. O Savior dear, who bore my sin, Who bled and died that I might win A glorious place in heav'n above, aI'll praise Thy wondrous love.
2. Give me more strength, I humbly pray, To walk the straight and narrow way, To bear my cross, what e'er it be And put my trust in Thee.
3. Lord, fill my soul with radiant light, That I may love the cause of right; I'll do Thy will and shout Thy name To lift some soul from shame.
4. Oh, when my time shall come to go And leave all things on earth below; grant then that I Thy voice may hear, Rejoicing, Savior dear.

Isaiah 53:45

96 Our Savior

Rick Graham

Rick Graham

Our Sav - ior, in Geth - sem - a - ne Cried,
Our Sav - ior, whose hands raised the dead, Were
Our Sav - ior, bleed - ing on the tree, From
Our Sav - ior suf - fered all of these So
"Fa - ther, take this cup from me, But if Thou wilt, I'll
pierced with nails, His blood they shed. Sym - bol - ic of His
head and feet, and side flowed free. As sym - bols of His
that God's law He did ap - pease, We come to Him, our
drink it all"; A - ton - ing for our sins, and Fall
bo - dy torn, We eat the bread, our souls re - born.
blood, so dear, We now par - take the wa - ter clear.
hearts are rent, And we par - take His sac - ra - ment.

Luke 22:42

Our Savior in Gethsemane

Hyrum Mead | Hyrum Mead; arr. Rosemary Mead

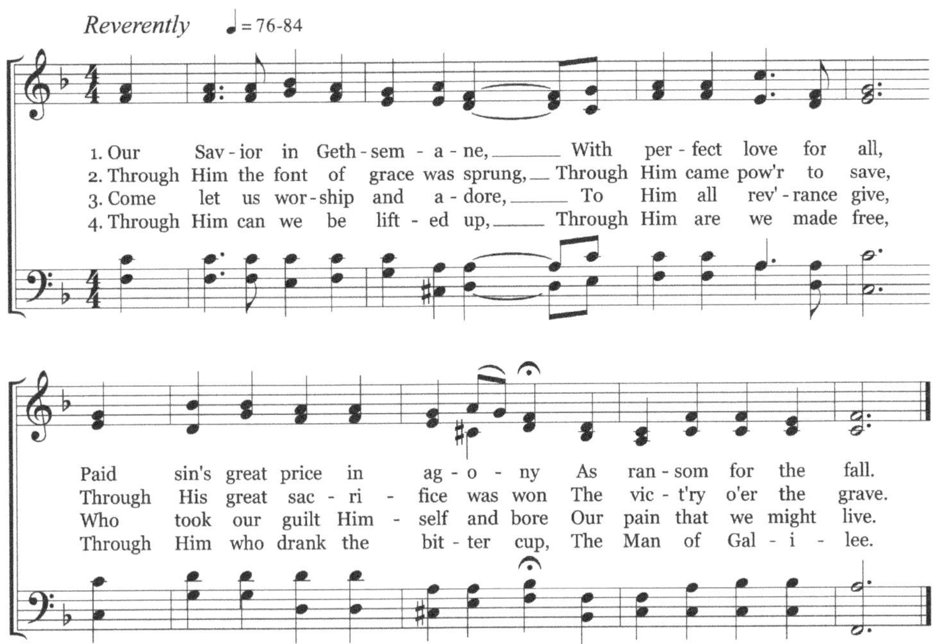
Reverently ♩ = 76-84
1. Our Sav - ior in Geth - sem - a - ne, With per - fect love for all,
2. Through Him the font of grace was sprung, Through Him came pow'r to save,
3. Come let us wor - ship and a - dore, To Him all rev' - rance give,
4. Through Him can we be lift - ed up, Through Him are we made free,
Paid sin's great price in ag - o - ny As ran - som for the fall.
Through His great sac - ri - fice was won The vic - t'ry o'er the grave.
Who took our guilt Him - self and bore Our pain that we might live.
Through Him who drank the bit - ter cup, The Man of Gal - i - lee.

5. 'Twas He who taught us sacrifice,
And how we should forgive,
Who gave Salvation without price,
And showed us how to live.

6. We take upon ourselves His name
And bear it reverently,
And filled with gladness we proclaim
The Man of Galilee!

Luke 22:42

98 Redeemed and Renewed

Sacrament Hymns

Michael D. Young

Melvyn R. Windham, Jr.

As though I ___ stand at wa - ter's edge, To be im - mersed be -
As through I ___ stand be - fore God's throne, To praise and wor - ship
neath the pool, I stand be - fore the Sac - ra - ment, And
to His face. I stand with - in His ho - ly house, A -
drink the wa - ter, pure and cool. Re - deemed and re-newed as I
light with heav - en's ho - ly grace. Re - deemed and re-newed as I
think of His blood, Im - mersed in the Spir - it that flows like a flood.
think of His light, And bask - ing in glo - ry so vi - brant and bright.

3 Nephi 19:10-11

99

Repentance

Sacrament Hymns

Hyrum Mead

Rosemary Mead

The heal - ing balm of grace from Thee, Re -
Lord, may I ev - er faith - ful be, Hold
There I will live in con - fi - dence Through
Thus I'll es - cape sin's aw - ful harms In -

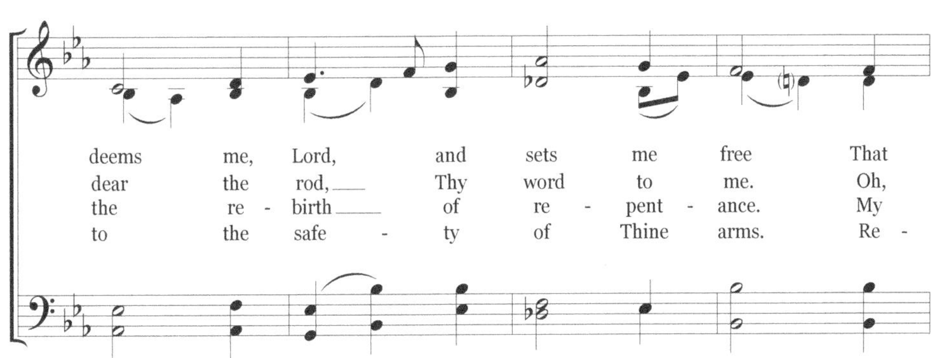
deems me, Lord, and sets me free That
dear the rod, Thy word to me. Oh,
the re - birth of re - pent - ance. My
to the safe - ty of Thine arms. Re -

I might yet ob - tain a place Where
guide me through these ways un - known Through
gar - ments washed, my lost soul won Through
deemed, I'll join heav'n's hosts to sing My

I may dwell be - fore Thy face.
dark - ened paths back to Thy home.
Thine a - tone - ment, cho - sen Son.
prais - es to Thee, glo - rious King.

Alma 42:22
Helaman 5:11

100

Sacrament

Sacrament Hymns

David Macfarlane and Nathan Howe
David Macfarlane arr. Nathan Howe
As we par-take of bro-ken bread Blessed by Thine au - thor - i -
As we par-take of wa - ter pure, We re - mem - ber Je - sus's
As we re - ceive this sac - ra - ment, Em - blems of His sac - ri -
ty, We con - tem-plate the Bread of Life, Slain for us on
blood, Which, fall - ing down from ev - 'ry pore, Made Him trem - ble,
fice, We cel - e - brate the emp - ty tomb, Em - blem of the
Cal - va - ry; And of - fer up our bro - ken hearts. Bless this
e - ven God. Though scar - let be our man - y sins, Make our
Liv - ing Christ. As hope re - claims our o - pen hearts, May the
sac - ri - fice we pray That we may em - u - late Thy
gar - ments white as snow Through Je - sus and His co - ve -
Spir - it sanc - ti - fy That when in glo - ry He ap -

Son, Ev - er will - ing to o - bey.
nant, Liv - ing wa - ter to our souls.
pears, We may have e - ter - nal life.

1 Corinthians 11:24-25
3 Nephi 18:11

101

The Last Supper

Sacrament Hymns

Kim L. Jensen

Kevin G. Pace

The streets were dark, the men were hushed who gath - ered 'round the
The qui - et of the gar - den soon re - placed by fear and
But the tomb; it could not hold Him! Tri - um - phant - ly He
Lord, The bread was bro - ken, the wine was sipped as they lis - tened to His
flight, The sol - i - tude of break - ing bread for - got - ten for that
came. He of - fers to re - deem us; His mer - cy we may
word. The dis - ci - ples, al - though wit - ness - es, had yet to see the
night. The hor - rors of Gol - go - tha; the shouts, the cross, the
claim. We hum - bly now be - fore Him bow; as wit - ness - es we
price, That soon there - af - ter would be paid through their Lord's sac - ri - fice.
nails; The bod - y placed with - in the tomb, the si - lenced wom-en's wails.
call On Je - sus, our dear Lord and God, the Sav - ior of us all.

Luke 22:12-19

102 White As Wool and Clean Again

Sacrament Hymns

Michael D. Young

Michael D. Young

I kneel be - fore Thy throne to - day. Send me
I see that I have wan - dered far. Be Thou
My heart is har - rowed by my wrong. A - wake
I stand be - fore Thee, new and pure. Beau - ty
trem - bling not a - way. My soul a tem - pest
now my guid - ing star. And I with spot - ted
now re - demp - tion's song. With joy as pure as
where the ash - es were. Re - newed, re - freshed and
deep with - in, Trou - bled by my ev - ery sin.
robes re - turn, Claim a gift I did not earn.
snow is white, Bring end to this bit - ter night.
rev - er - ent For this heal - ing, heav - en sent.
Lord, make this my scar - let stain white as wool and clean a - gain.

Isaiah 1:18

103 A Poor Wayfaring Man of Grief

New Settings

James Montgomery

George Coles, arr. Michael D. Young

A poor way - far - ing man of grief Hath of - ten
I spied him where a foun - tain burst Clear from the
In pris'n I saw him next con - demned To meet a
Then in a mo - ment to my view, The strang - er

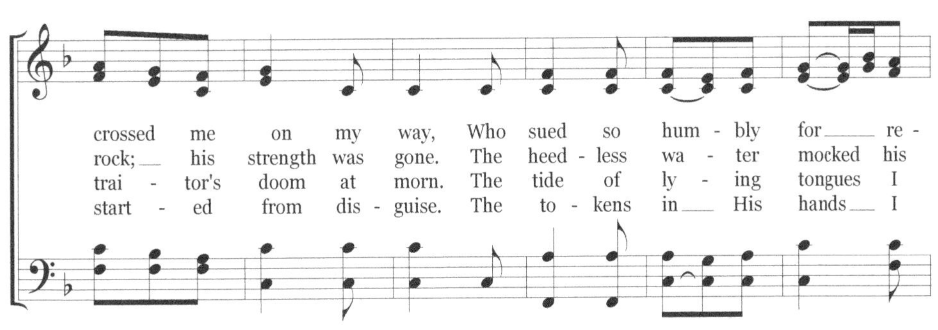
crossed me on my way, Who sued so hum - bly for re -
rock; his strength was gone. The heed - less wa - ter mocked his
trai - tor's doom at morn. The tide of ly - ing tongues I
start - ed from dis - guise. The to - kens in His hands I

lief That I could nev - er an - swer nay. I had not
thirst. He heard it, saw it hur - rying on. I ran and
stemmed And hon - ored him 'mid shame and scorn. My friend - ship's
knew; The Sav - ior stood be - fore my eyes. He spake and

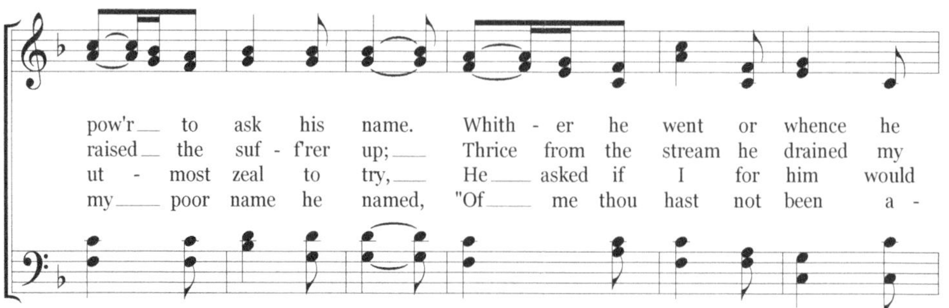

pow'r to ask his name. Whith - er he went or whence he
raised the suf - f'rer up; Thrice from the stream he drained my
ut - most zeal to try, He asked if I for him would
my poor name he named, "Of me thou hast not been a -

came. But there was some - thing in his
cup, Dipped and re - turned it run - ning
die. The flesh was weak, my blood ran
shamed. These deeds shall thy me - mo - rial

eye That won my love I knew not why.
o'er. I drank and ne - ver thirst - ed more.
chill, But my free spir - it cried, "I will."
be. Fear not, thou didst them un - to me."

Matthew 25:31-40
Mosiah 2:17

104 Behold the Great Redeemer Die

New Settings

Eliza R. Snow
John C. Leavitt
Be - hold the great Re - deem-er die, A bro - ken law to sat - is - fy. He dies a sac - ri - fice for sin, That man may live and glo - ry win.
While guilt - y men His pains de - ride, They pierce His hands and feet and side; And with in - sult - ing scoffs and scorns, They crown His head with plait-ed thorns.
Al - though in ag - o - ny He hung, no mur - m'ring word es - caped His tongue. His high com - mis - sion to ful - fill, He mag - ni - fied His Fa - ther's will.
"Fa - ther, from me re - move this cup. Yet, if Thou wilt, I'll drink it up. I've done the work Thou gav - est me. Re - ceive my spir - it un - to Thee."
1, 2, 3, 4, 5.
(interlude)
6.
Doctrine and Covenants 18:11
Luke 22:42

5. He died, and at the awful sight
The sun in shame withdrew its light!
Earth trembled, and all nature sighed,
In dread response, "A God has died!"

6. He lives--he lives. We humbly now
Around these sacred symbols bow,
And seek, as Saints of latter days,
To do His will and live His praise.

105
New Settings

Christ the Lord Is Risen Today

Charles Wesley

Robert Williams, arr. Michael D. Young

Christ the Lord is ris'n to - day, Al - le - lu - ia!
Love's re - deem - ing work is ___ done. Al - le - lu - ia!
Lives a - gain, our glor - ious King. Al - le - lu - ia!

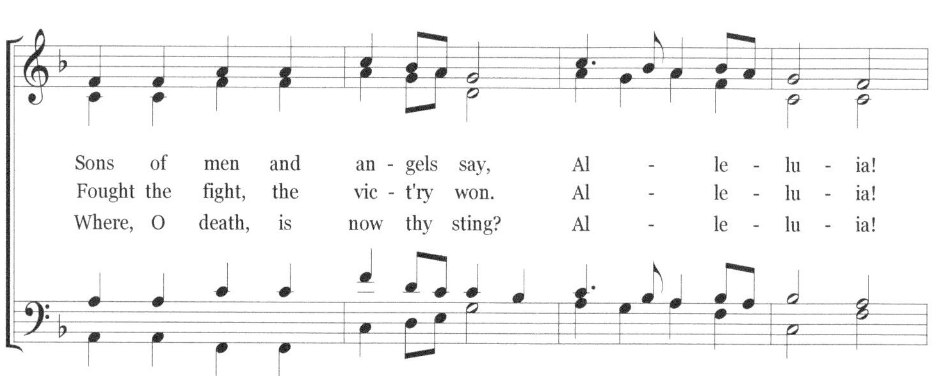
Sons of men and an - gels say, Al - le - lu - ia!
Fought the fight, the vic - t'ry won. Al - le - lu - ia!
Where, O death, is now thy sting? Al - le - lu - ia!

Raise your joys and tri - umphs high, Al - le - lu - ia!
Je - sus's ag - on - y ___ is ___ o'er. Al - le lu ia!
Once He died our souls to ___ save. Al - le - lu - ia!

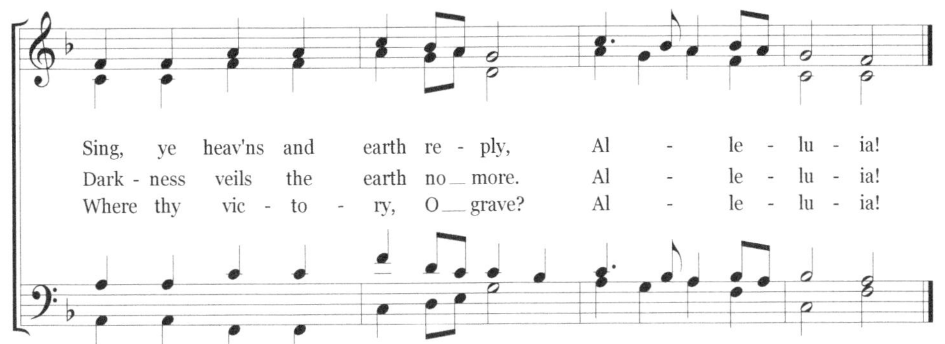

Sing, ye heav'ns and earth re - ply, Al - le - lu - ia!
Dark - ness veils the earth no more. Al - le - lu - ia!
Where thy vic - to - ry, O grave? Al - le - lu - ia!

Matthew 28:5-6
1 Corinthians 15:20, 53-57

106 Come, Follow Me

New Settings

John Nicholson

Thomas Tallis, arr. Brent Yorgason

"Come, fol - low me," the Sav - ior said. Then let us in His
"Come, fol - low me," a sim - ple phrase, Yet truth's sub - lime, ef -
Is it e - nough a - lone to know That we must fol - low
Not on - ly shall we em - u - late His course while in this
"Come, fol - low me," the Sav - ior said. Then
"Come, fol - low me," a sim - ple phrase, Yet
Is it e - nough a - lone to know That
Not on - ly shall we em - u - late His
foot - steps tread, For thus a - lone can we be one With
ful - gent rays Are in these sim - ple words com - bined To
Him be - low, While trav - 'ling thru this vale of tears? No,
earth - ly state, But when we're freed from pres - ent cares, If
let us in His foot - steps tread, For thus a - lone can
truth's sub - lime, ef - ful - gent rays Are in these sim - ple
we must fol - low Him be - low, While trav - 'ling thru this
course while in this earth - ly state, But when we're freed from

God's own loved, be - got - ten Son.
urge, in - spire the hu - man mind.
this ex - tends to ho - lier spheres.
with our Lord we would be heirs.
we be one With God's own loved, be - got - ten Son.
words com - bined To urge, in - spire the hu - man mind.
vale of tears? No, this ex - tends to ho - lier spheres.
pres - ent cares, If with our Lord we would be heirs.

Matthew 4:19
2 Nephi 31:10-21

107 Come Unto Jesus

New Settings

Orson Pratt Huish

Rebecca Belliston

Come un - to Je - sus, ye heav - y la - den, Care - worn and
Come un - to Je - sus, He'll sure - ly hear you, If you in
Come un - to Je - sus, He'll ev - er heed you, Though in the
faint - ing, by sin op - pressed. He'll safe - ly guide you
meek - ness plead for His love. Oh, know you not that
dark - ness you've gone a - stray. His love will find you
un - to that ha - ven Where all who trust Him may rest.
an - gels are near you From bright - est man - sions a - bove?
and gent - ly lead you From dark - est night in - to day.

Matthew 11:28-30
2 Nephi 26:33

108 Dearest Children, God Is Near You

New Settings

Charles L. Walker and Michael D. Young

Shaker Folk Song, arr. Michael D. Young

Dear - est child-ren, God is near you watch - ing o'er you day _ and night,
Dear - est child-ren, ho - ly an - gels watch your ac - tions night and day,
Child-ren, God de - lights to teach you by His Ho - ly Spir - it's voice.
Dear - est child-ren, God will ev - er dry your tears as with His
And de - lights to own and bless you if you strive to do _ what's right.
And they keep a faith - ful re - cord of the good and bad you say.
Quick - ly heed its ho - ly prompt-ings. Day by day you'll then re - joice.
For His Son did bear your bur - den. All your grief He felt a - lone.
He will bless you! He will bless you! If you put your trust in Him.
Cher - ish vir - tue! Cher - ish vir - tue! God will bless the pure in heart.
Oh, prove faith - ful, oh, prove faith - ful! to your God and Zi - on's cause.
Oh, prove thank - ful, oh, prove thank - ful! to your God and to His Son!
He will bless you! He will bless you! If you put your trust in Him.
Cher - ish vir - tue! Cher - ish vir - tue! God will bless the pure in heart.
Oh, prove faith - ful, oh, prove faith - ful! to your God and Zi - on's cause.
Oh, prove thank - ful, oh, prove thank - ful! to your God and to His Son!

Psalms 37:3-5
Doctrine and Covenants 76:5

109
New Settings

For the Beauty of the Earth

Foilliot S. Pierpoint

Henry J. Gauntlet, arr. Michael D. Young

For the beau - ty of the earth, For the beau - ty of the skies,
For the beau - ty of each hour Of the day and of the night,
For the joy of hu - man love, Broth - er, sis - ter, par - ent, child,
For the love which from our birth Ov - er and a - round us lies,
Hill and vale and tree and flow'r, Sun and moon, and stars of light,
Friends on earth, and friends a - bove, For all gen - tle thoughts and mild,
Lord of to Thee we raise This our hymn of grate - ful praise.

Psalms 95:1-6
Psalms 33:1-6

110 Hark, All Ye Nations

New Settings

Louis F. Moench

Phoebe P. Knapp, arr. Michael D. Young

Hark, all ye na - tions, Hear hea - ven's voice
Search - ing in dark - ness, Na - tions have wept;
Chos - en by God to Serv Him be - low,
To ev - 'ry land that all may re - joice.
Watch - ing for dawn, their vi - gil they've kept.
To ev - 'ry land and peo - ple we'll go,
An - gels of glo - ry shout the re - frain:
All now re - joice; the long night is o'er.
Stand - ing for truth with fer - vent ac - cord,
Truth is re - stored a - gain.
Truth is on earth once more!
Teach - ing His ho - ly word.

Oh, how glo - rious from a - bove
Shines the gos - pel light of love.

Bright as the sun this heav-en-ly ray
Lights ev - 'ry land to-day!

Doctrine and Covenants 133:36-38
Doctrine and Covenants 128:19-21

Alternate Text: (Fanny Crosby)

1. Blessed assurance, Jesus is mine!
Oh, what a foretaste of glory divine!
Heir of salvation, purchase of God,
Born of His Spirit, washed in His blood.

Refrain:
This is my story, this is my song,
praising my Savior all the day long;
this is my story, this is my song,
praising my Savior all the day long.

2. Perfect submission, perfect delight!
Visions of rapture now burst on my sight;
Angels descending bring from above
Echoes of mercy, whispers of love.

(Refrain)

3. Perfect submission, all is at rest!
I in my Savior am happy and blessed,
Watching and waiting, looking above,
Filled with His goodness, lost in His love.

(Refrain)

111 Have I Done Any Good?

New Settings

Will L. Thompson

Traditional Hymn, arr. Brent Yorgason

Have I done an - y good in the world to - day? Have I
Has an - y - one's bur - den been light - er to - day Be -
There are chanc - es for work all a - round just now, Op - por-
'Tis no - ble of man to work and to give; Love's
helped an - y - one in need? (one in need) Have I
cause I was will - ing to share? (to share) Have the
tu - ni - ties right in our way. (in our way) Do not
la - bor has mer - it a - lone. (a - lone) On - ly
cheered up the sad and made some - one feel glad? If
sick and the wea - ry been helped on their way? When they
let them pass by, say - ing, "Some - time I'll try," But
he who does some - thing helps oth - ers to live. To

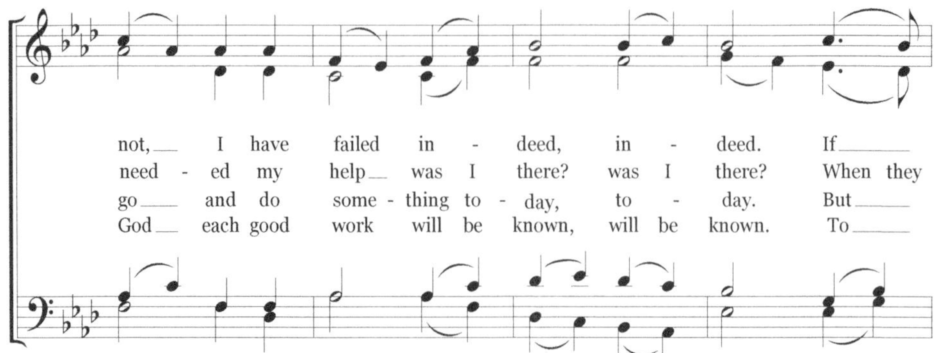
not, I have failed in - deed, in - deed. If
need - ed my help was I there? was I there? When they
go and do some - thing to - day, to - day. But
God each good work will be known, will be known. To

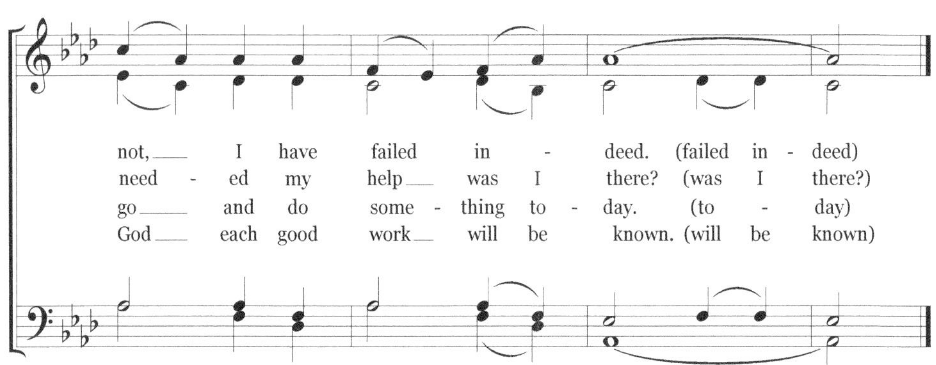
not, I have failed in - deed. (failed in - deed)
need - ed my help was I there? (was I there?)
go and do some - thing to - day. (to - day)
God each good work will be known. (will be known)

James 1:22
Alma 9:28

112 How Gentle God's Commands

New Settings

Phillip Doldridge

Jonathan C. Woodman, arr. Brent Yorgason

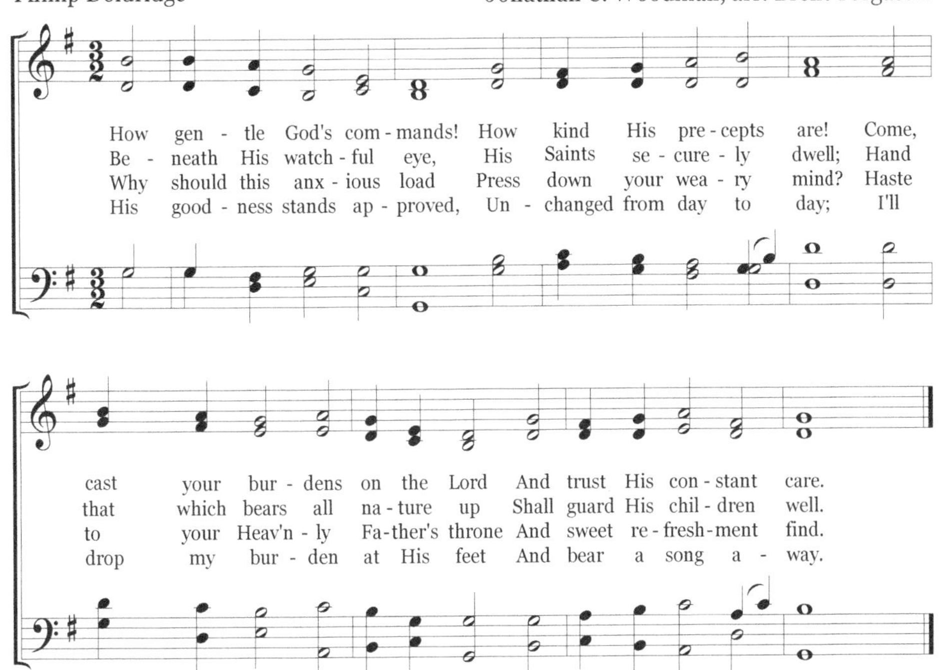
How gen - tle God's com - mands! How kind His pre - cepts are! Come,
Be - neath His watch - ful eye, His Saints se - cure - ly dwell; Hand
Why should this anx - ious load Press down your wea - ry mind? Haste
His good - ness stands ap - proved, Un - changed from day to day; I'll
cast your bur - dens on the Lord And trust His con - stant care.
that which bears all na - ture up Shall guard His chil - dren well.
to your Heav'n - ly Fa - ther's throne And sweet re - fresh - ment find.
drop my bur - den at His feet And bear a song a - way.

1 John 5:3
Psalms 55:22

113

New Settings

I Need Thee Every Hour

Anne S. Hawks

Norwegian Folk Song arr. Michael D. Young

I need Thee ev - 'ry hour, most gra - cious Lord! No ten - der voice like Thine can peace af - ford.
I need Thee ev - 'ry hour, stay Thou near - by. Temp - ta - tions lose their pow'r when Thou art nigh.
I need Thee ev - 'ry hour, in joy or pain. Come quick - ly and a - bide or life is vain.
I need Thee ev - 'ry hour, Most Ho - ly One! Oh, make me Thine in - deed, Thou bless - ed Son!
I need Thee, oh, I need Thee! Ev-'ry hour I need Thee. Oh, bless me now, my Sav - ior. I come to

2 Nephi 4:16-35
Psalms 143:1

114

New Settings

I Saw a Mighty Angel Fly

Anon. Oliver Holden, arr. Michael D. Young

I saw a might - y an - gel fly; To earth he bent his
Truth is the mes - sage which he bears: the gos - pel's joy - ful
He cries, and with a might - y voice; Ye na - tions lend an
He cries; let ev - 'ry ear at - tend, and thrones and em-pires
way, to earth he bent his way, A mes - sage bear - ing from on
sound, the gos - pel's joy - ful sound, To calm our hearts to chase our
ear, ye na - tions lend an ear, And isles and con - ti - nents re -
all, and thrones and em - pires all. Fear God, and make the Lord your
high to cheer us. Cheer us,
fears and make our joys. Our joys,
joice: the great Re - deem - er, Great Re -
friend, the King, and Lord of all. The King,
cheer us, Cheer to cheer the sons of day.
our joys, Our joys, to make our joys a - bound.
deem - er, The great Re - dee - mer now is here!
the King, The King and Lord, the Lord of all!

Revelation 14:6-7
Doctrine and Covenants 133:39, 52-53

115

New Settings

I Stand All Amazed

Charles H. Gabriel

American Folk Song, arr. Michael D. Young

I stand all a - mazed at the love Je - sus of - fers me; con - fused at the grace He prof - fers me! I trem - ble to know that for me He was cru - ci - fied, that for me a sin - ner He suf - fered, bled, and died.
I mar - vel that He would de - scend from His throne di - vine to res - cue a soul so re - bel - ious, mine! That He would ex - tend His great love un - to such as I, suf - fi - cient to own to re - deem, to jus - ti - fy.
I think of His hands pierced and bleed - ing to pay the debt, such mer - cy, such love, can I for - get? No, no, I will praise and a - dore at the mer - cy seat, un - til at His throne I kneel at His feet.
Oh, it is won - der - ful that He should care for me, e nough to die for me!

Oh, it is won-der-ful that He should care for me. It is won-der-ful, won-der-ful to me.

Mosiah 3:5-8
John 15:13

116 I'll Go Where You Want Me to Go

New Settings

Mary Brown

Brent Yorgason

It___ may not be on the moun - tain height Or
Per - haps to - day there are lov - ing words Which
There's sure - ly some - where a low - ly place In

o - ver the storm - y sea, It may not be at the
Je - sus would have me speak; There may be now in the
earth's har - vest fields so wide Where I may la - bor through

bat - tle's front My Lord will have need of me. But
paths of sin Some wan - d'rer whom I should seek. O
life's short day For Je - sus, the Cru - ci - fied. So

if, by a still, small voice He calls To paths that I do not know, I'll
Sav - ior, if Thou wilt be my guide, Tho dark and rug - ged the way, My
trust - ing my all to Thy ten - der care, And know - ing Thou lov - est me, I'll

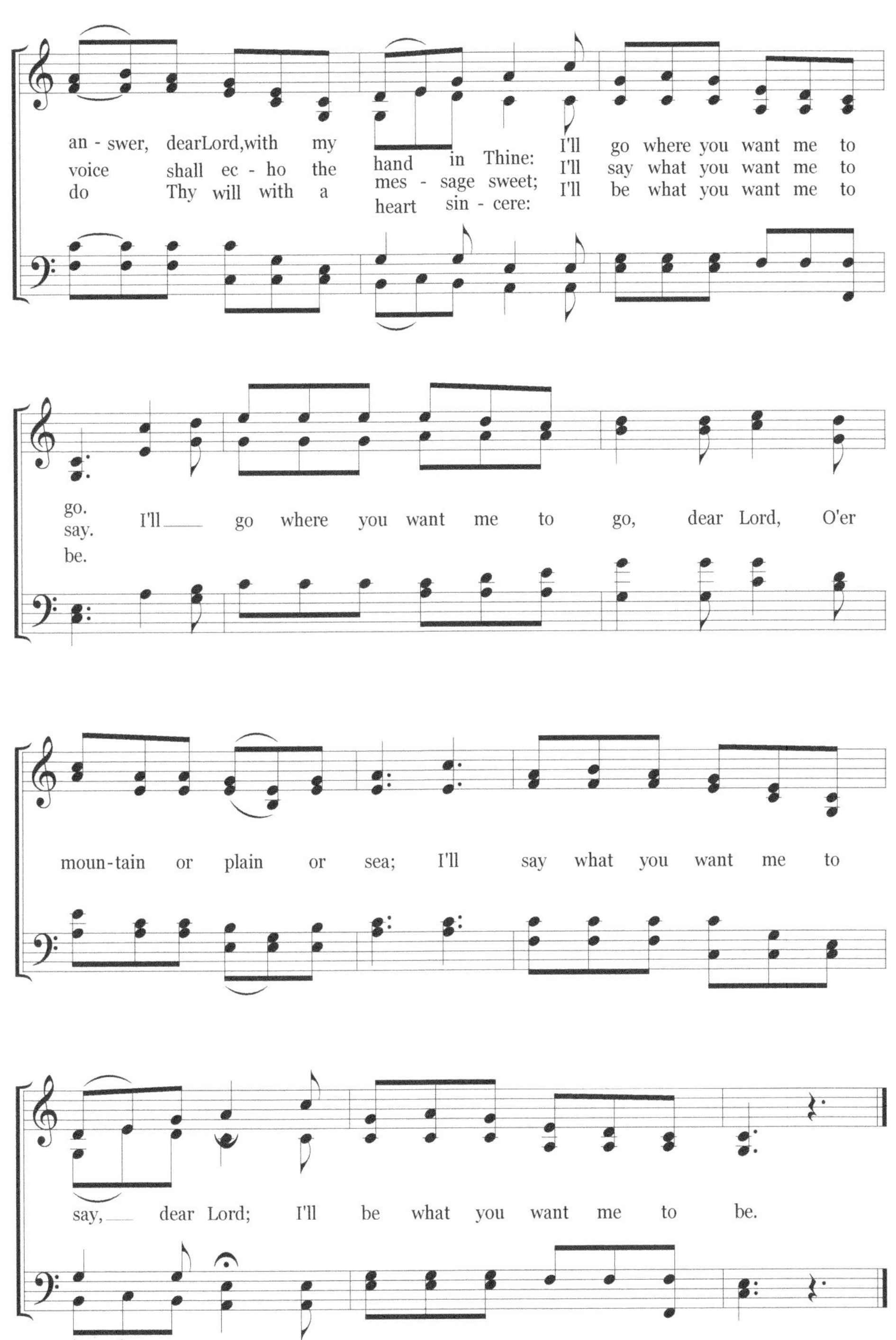
an - swer, dear Lord, with my hand in Thine: I'll go where you want me to go.
voice shall ec - ho the mes - sage sweet; I'll say what you want me to say.
do Thy will with a heart sin - cere: I'll be what you want me to be.
I'll go where you want me to go, dear Lord, O'er
moun-tain or plain or sea; I'll say what you want me to
say, dear Lord; I'll be what you want me to be.

Text © 2015 Mary Brown
Music © 2015 Brent Yorgason

1 Nephi 3:7
Luke 12:37

117

I'm a Pilgrim, I'm a Stranger

New Settings

Henry Petersen

Jared Bernotski

I'm a pil - grim, I'm a strang - er Cast up - on the rock - y
va - pors rise be - fore me; Scarce-ly can I see the
Fa - ther, I en - treat Thee, Let me see Thy beck - 'ning
shore Of a land where death - ly dan - ger Sur - ges with a sul - len
way. Clouds of dark - est hue hang o - 'er me, And I'm apt to go a -
hand, And when stray - ing may I meet Thee Ere I join the si - lent
roar. Oft de - spair - ing, oft de - spair - ing, Lest I reach my home no
stray. With the man - y with the man - y, That are now the vul - ture's
band. Guide me, Fa - ther guide me, Fa - ther, safe - ly to the prom - ised
more. Oft de - spair - ing, oft de - spair - ing, Lest I
prey. With the man - y, with the man - y, That are
land. Guide me, Fa - ther, guide me Fa - ther, safe - ly

1
2
3.
reach my home no more. Mist-y
prey. O my
now the vul-ture's
to the prom-ised land.

Music © Jared Bernotski

Hebrews 11:12-16

118 In Hymns of Praise

New Settings

Ada Blenkhorn

Gustav Holst, arr. Brent Yorgason

In hymns of praise your voic - es raise To Him who reigns on high, Whose
The lit - tle flow'r that lasts an hour, The spar - row in its fall, They,
coun - sels keep the might - y deep, Who rul - eth earth and sky. Be -
too, shall share His ten - der care; He made and loves them all. Then
neath His hand, at His com - mand, The shin - ing plan - ets move; To
sing a - gain in loft - y strain To Him who dwells on high; To
all be - low they dai - ly show His wis - dom and His love. Ex -
prayers you raise, and songs of praise, He sweet - ly will re - ply.

alt His name in loud ac-claim; His might-y pow'r a - dore! And
hum - bly bow be-fore Him now, Our King for-ev - er - more.

1 Chronicles 16:29
Matthew 10:29-31

119 Jesus, the Very Thought of Thee

New Settings

Bernard of Clairvaux trans. Edward Caswall

Jeff Kocherhans

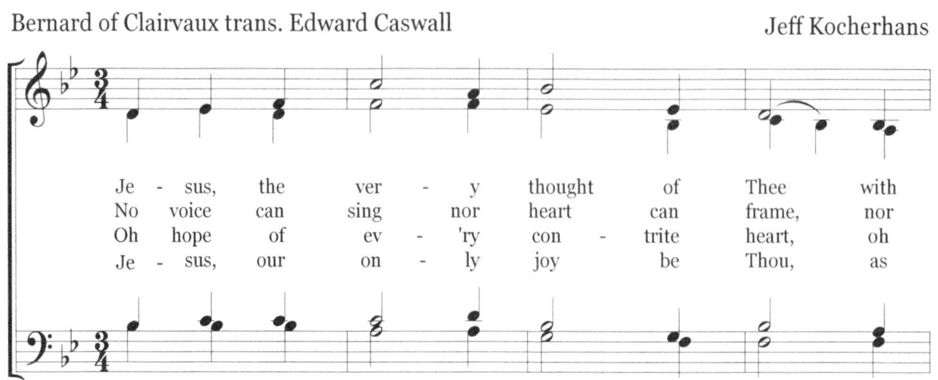
Je - sus, the ver - y thought of Thee with
No voice can sing nor heart can frame, nor
Oh hope of ev - 'ry con - trite heart, oh
Je - sus, our on - ly joy be Thou, as

sweet - ness fills my breast.
can the mem - 'ry find
joy of all the meek,
Thou our prize wilt be.

But sweet - er far Thy face to see,
A sweet - er sound than Thy blest name,
To those who fall, how kind Thou art,
Je - sus, be Thou our glo - ry now,

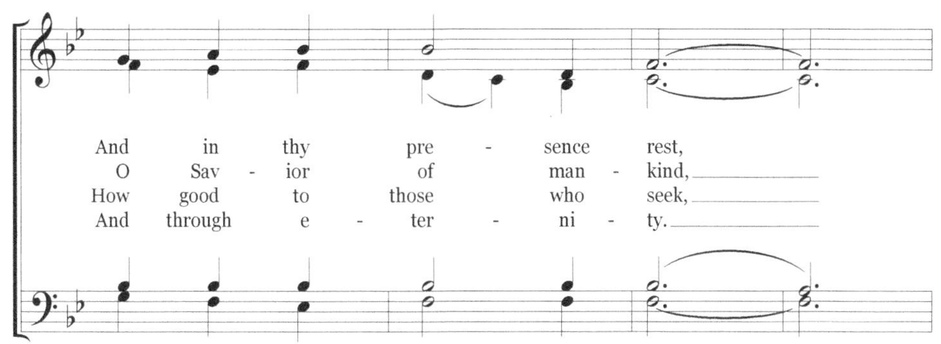
And in thy pre - sence rest,
O Sav - ior of man - kind,
How good to those who seek,
And through e - ter - ni - ty.

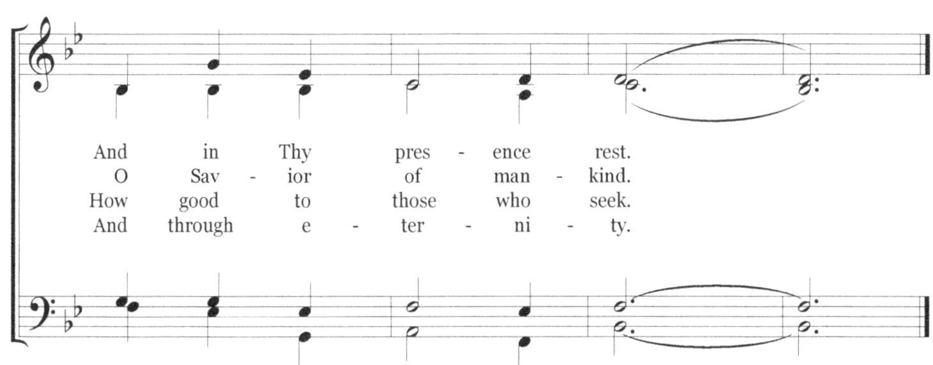
And in Thy pres - ence rest.
O Sav - ior of man - kind.
How good to those who seek.
And through e - ter - ni - ty.

Psalms 104:34
Enos 1:27

120 Joseph Smith's First Prayer

New Settings

George Manwaring

Gustav Holst, arr. Michael D. Young

Oh, how love - ly was the mor - ning! Ra - diant beamed the sun a -
Hum - bly kneel - ing, sweet ap - peal - ing 'twas the boy's first ut - tered
Sud - den - ly a light de - scend - ed, bright - er far than noon - day
"Jo - seph, this is my Be - lov - ed; Hear Him!" Oh, how sweet the

bove. Bees were hum - ming, sweet birds sing - ing, mu - sic ring - ing through the
prayer When the pow'rs of sin as - sail - ing filled his soul with deep de -
sun, And a shin - ing, glo - rious pil - lar o'er him fell, a - round him
word! Jo - seph's hum - ble prayer was an - swered, and he lis - tened to the

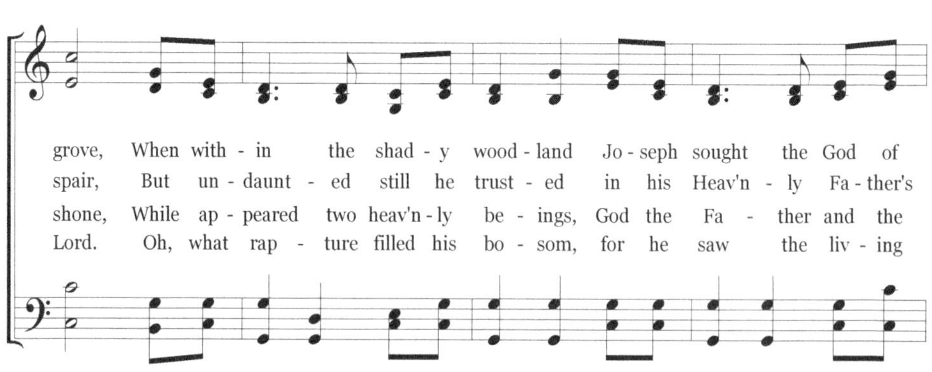

grove, When with - in the shad - y wood - land Jo - seph sought the God of
spair, But un - daunt - ed still he trust - ed in his Heav'n - ly Fa - ther's
shone, While ap - peared two heav'n - ly be - ings, God the Fa - ther and the
Lord. Oh, what rap - ture filled his bo - som, for he saw the liv - ing

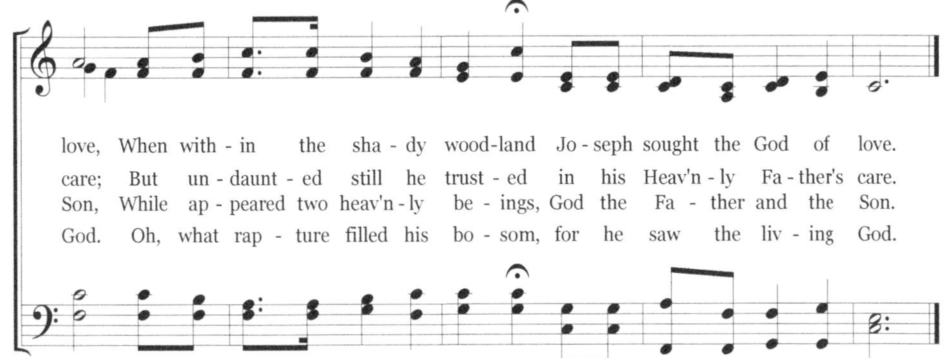
love, When with - in the sha - dy wood-land Jo - seph sought the God of love.
care; But un - daunt - ed still he trust - ed in his Heav'n - ly Fa - ther's care.
Son, While ap - peared two heav'n - ly be - ings, God the Fa - ther and the Son.
God. Oh, what rap - ture filled his bo - som, for he saw the liv - ing God.

Joseph Smith—History 1:14–20, 25
James 1:5

121

Let Us All Press On

New Settings

Evan Stephens

Frederic F. Bullard arr. Brent Yorgason

Let us all press on in the work of the Lord, That when
We will not re - treat, though our numbers may be few When com -
If we do what's right we have no need to fear, For the
life is o'er we may gain a re - ward; In the
pared with the op - po - site host in view; But an
Lord, our help - er, will ev - er be near; In the
fight for right let us wield a sword, The
un - seen pow'r will aid me and you In the
days of trial His Saints He will cheer, And
might - y sword of truth.
glo - rious cause of truth.
pros - per the cause of truth.

1 Nephi 22:15-17
2 Nephi 31:20

122 Nearer, My God, to Thee

New Settings

Sarah F. Adams

Folk Song, arr. Michael D. Young

Near - er, my God, to Thee, Near - er to Thee.
Though like a wan - der - er, The sun gone down,
There let the way ap - pear, Steps un - to heav'n;
Then with my wak - ing thoughts, Bright with Thy praise,
Or if, on joy - ful wing Cleav - ing the sky,
E'en though it be a cross That rais - eth me. Still
Dark - ness be o - ver me, My rest a stone. Yet
All that thou send - est me, In mer - cy giv'n; An -
Out of my ston - y griefs Beth - el I'll raise; So
Sun, moon, and stars for - got, Up - ward I fly, Still
all, still all my song shall be Near -
in, yet in my dreams, I'd be
gels, An - gels to beck - on me
by, so by my woes to be
all, still all my song shall be
er, my God, to Thee, near - er to Thee! To Thee!

Doctrine and Covenants 88:63
Genesis 28:10-22

123

New Settings

O My Father

Eliza R. Snow

Marta Keen arr. Michael D. Young

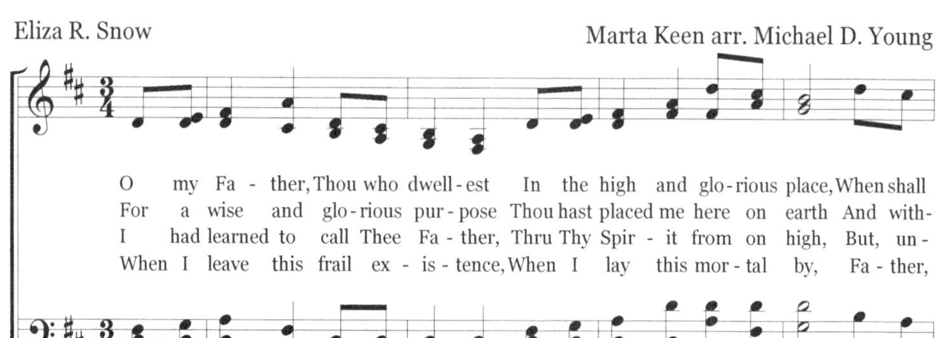
O my Fa - ther, Thou who dwell - est In the high and glo - rious place, When shall
For a wise and glo - rious pur - pose Thou hast placed me here on earth And with -
I had learned to call Thee Fa - ther, Thru Thy Spir - it from on high, But, un -
When I leave this frail ex - is - tence, When I lay this mor - tal by, Fa - ther,

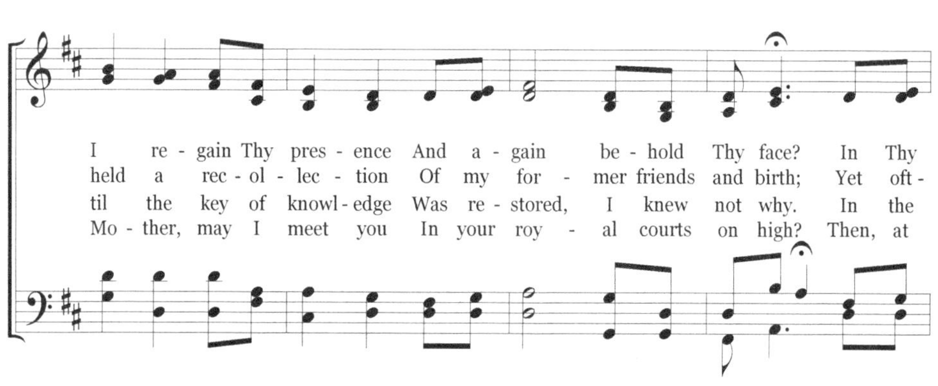
I re - gain Thy pres - ence And a - gain be - hold Thy face? In Thy
held a rec - ol - lec - tion Of my for - mer friends and birth; Yet oft -
til the key of knowl - edge Was re - stored, I knew not why. In the
Mo - ther, may I meet you In your roy - al courts on high? Then, at

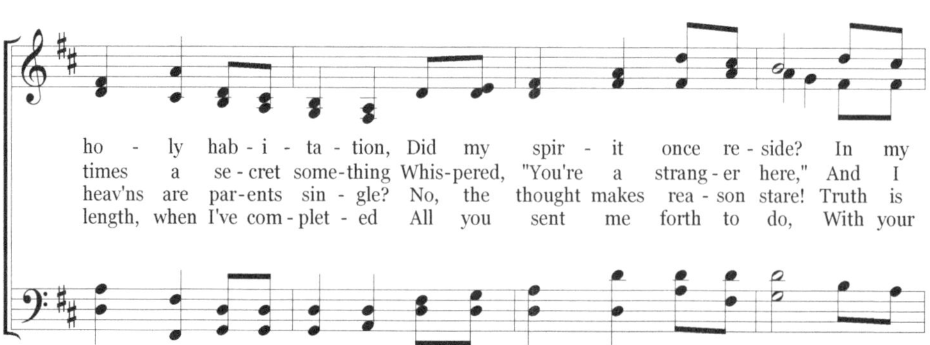
ho - ly hab - i - ta - tion, Did my spir - it once re - side? In my
times a se - cret some - thing Whis - pered, "You're a strang - er here," And I
heav'ns are par - ents sin - gle? No, the thought makes rea - son stare! Truth is
length, when I've com - plet - ed All you sent me forth to do, With your

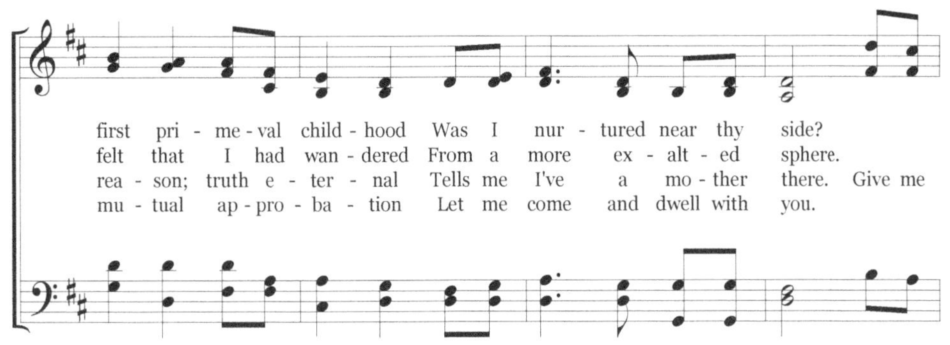
first pri - me - val child - hood Was I nur - tured near thy side?
felt that I had wan - dered From a more ex - alt - ed sphere.
rea - son; truth e - ter - nal Tells me I've a mo - ther there. Give me
mu - tual ap - pro - ba - tion Let me come and dwell with you.

rest in Thy pas - ture when my work here is through. Set me

free from tears and sigh - ing and let me come and dwell with you!

Luke 23: 53-56
Luke 24:1-9

124 Praise to the Man

New Settings

William W. Phelps

Traditional Tune, arr. Michael D. Young

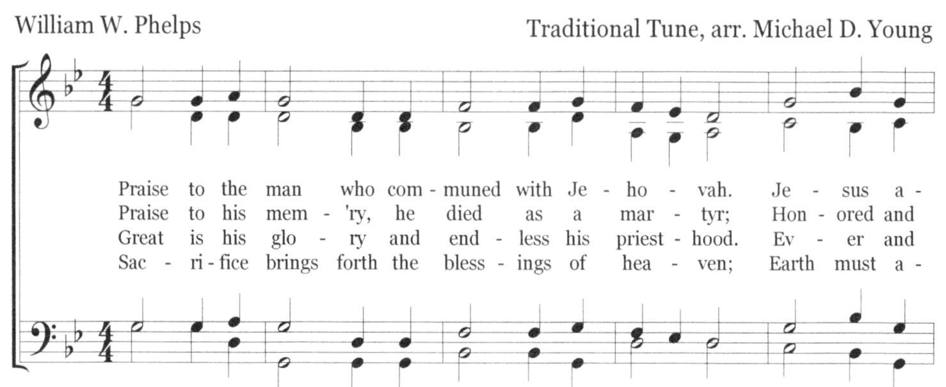
Praise to the man who com - muned with Je - ho - vah. Je - sus a -
Praise to his mem - 'ry, he died as a mar - tyr; Hon - ored and
Great is his glo - ry and end - less his priest - hood. Ev - er and
Sac - ri - fice brings forth the bless - ings of hea - ven; Earth must a -

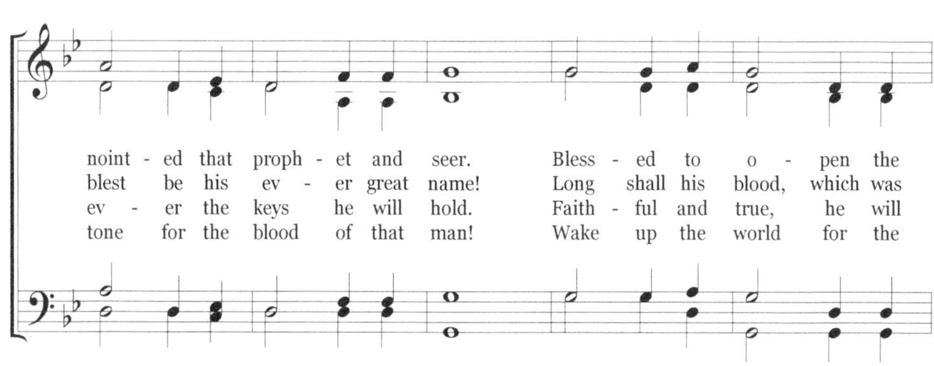
noint - ed that proph - et and seer. Bless - ed to o - pen the
blest be his ev - er great name! Long shall his blood, which was
ev - er the keys he will hold. Faith - ful and true, he will
tone for the blood of that man! Wake up the world for the

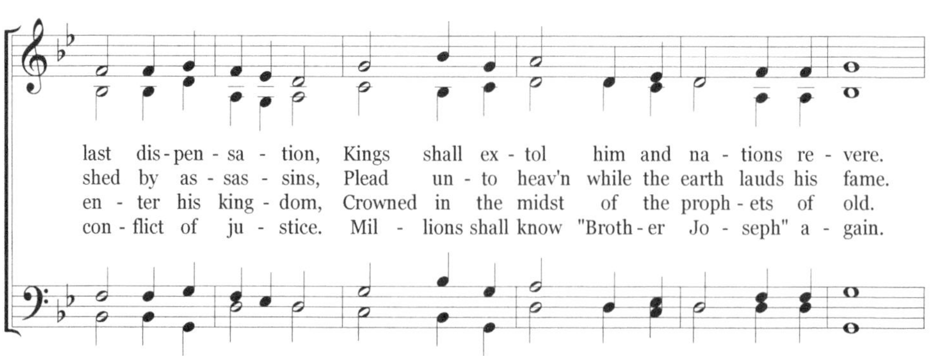
last dis - pen - sa - tion, Kings shall ex - tol him and na - tions re - vere.
shed by as - sas - sins, Plead un - to heav'n while the earth lauds his fame.
en - ter his king - dom, Crowned in the midst of the proph - ets of old.
con - flict of ju - stice. Mil - lions shall know "Broth - er Jo - seph" a - gain.

Hail to the proph - et, a - scend - ed to hea - ven! Trai - tors and

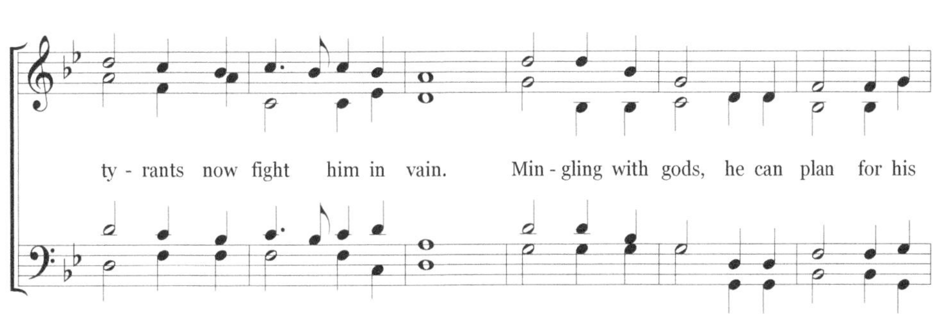
ty - rants now fight him in vain. Min - gling with gods, he can plan for his

breth - ren. Death can - not con - quer the he - ro a - gain!

Doctrine and Covenants 135
2 Nephi 3:14-15

125
New Settings

Precious Savior, Dear Redeemer

H. R. Palmer

Francois H. Barthelemon, arr. Brent Yorgason

Pre - cious Sav - ior, dear Re-deem - er, Thy sweet mes - sage now im -
Pre - cious Sav - ior, dear Re-deem - er, We are weak but Thou art
Pre - cious Sav - ior, dear Re-deem - er, Thou wilt bind the bro - ken
part. May Thy Spir - it, pure and fer - vid, En - ter ev - 'ry tim - id
strong; In Thy in - fi - nite com-pas - sion, Stay the tide of sin and
heart. Let not sor - row o - ver-whelm us; Dry the bit - ter tears that
heart; Car - ry there the swift con-vic - tion, Turn - ing back the sin - ful
wrong. Keep Thy lov - ing arms a-round us; Keep us in the nar-row
start. Curb the winds and calm the bil - lows; Bid the an - gry tem-pest
tide. Pre-cious Sav - ior, dear Re-deem-er, May each soul in Thee a - bide.
way. Pre-cious Sav - ior, dear Re-deem-er, Let us nev - er from Thee stray.
cease. Pre-cious Sav - ior, dear Re-deem-er, Grant us ev - er-last - ing peace.

Isaiah 26:3-4
Psalm 145:8-9

126

Put Your Shoulder to the Wheel

New Settings

Will L. Thompson

Brent Yorgason

The world has need of will - ing men Who wear the work - er's
The Church has need of help - ing hands, And hearts that know and
Then don't stand id - ly look - ing on; The fight with sin is
Then work and watch and fight and pray With all your might and
seal. Come, help the good work move a - long; Put your shoul-der to the wheel.
feel. The work to do is here for you; Put your shoul-der to the wheel.
real. It will be long but must go on; Put your shoul-der to the wheel.
zeal. Push ev - 'ry wor - thy work a - long; Put your shoul-der to the wheel.
Put your shoul-der to the wheel, put your shoul-der to the wheel, put your
shoul-der to the wheel, push a - long.
Put your shoul-der to the wheel; put your

shoul - der to the wheel, put your shoul-der to the wheel, push a - long.

Doctrine and Covenants 58:26-28
Doctrine and Covenants 107:99

Reverently and Meekly Now

New Settings

Joseph L. Townsend — Jeff Kocherhans

Rev - 'rent - ly and meek - ly now, Let thy head most hum - bly
In this bread now blessed for thee Em - blem of my bod - y
Bid thine heart all strife to cease; With thy breath - ren be at
At the throne I in - ter - cede; For thee ev - er do I

bow. Think of me, thou ran - somed one. Think what I for thee have
see. In this wa - ter or this wine Em - blem of my blood di -
peace. Oh, for - give as thou wouldst be E'en for - giv - en now by
plead. I have loved thee as thy friend With a love that can - not

done. With my blood that dripped like rain, Sweat in ag - o - ny of
vine. Oh, re - mem - ber what was done That the sin - ner might be
me. In the sol - emn faith of prayer Cast up - on me all thy
end. Be o - be - dient, I im - plore, Prayer - ful watch - ful, e - ver -

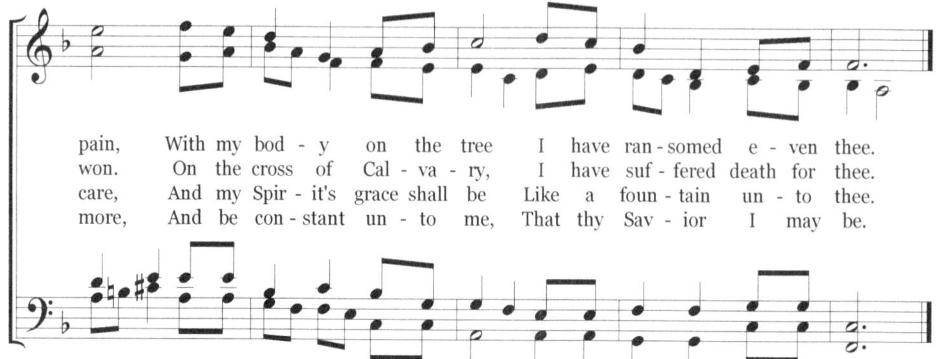
pain, With my bod - y on the tree I have ran - somed e - ven thee.
won. On the cross of Cal - va - ry, I have suf - fered death for thee.
care, And my Spir - it's grace shall be Like a foun - tain un - to thee.
more, And be con - stant un - to me, That thy Sav - ior I may be.

Doctrine and Covenants 45:3-5

Sweet Is the Work

Isaac Watts

Isaac B. Woodbury, arr. Brent Yorgason

Sweet is the work, my God, my King, To praise Thy name, give thanks and sing. To show Thy love by morn - ing light, And talk of all Thy truths at night.
Sweet is the day of sa - cred rest. No mor - tal care shall seize my breast. Oh, may my heart in tune be found, Like Da - vid's harp of sol - emn sound!
My heart shall tri - umph in my Lord And bless His works and bless His word. Thy works of grace, how bright they shine! How deep Thy coun - sels, how di - vine!
But, oh, what tri - umph shall I raise To Thy dear name through end - less days, When in the realms of joy I see Thy face in full fe - lic - i - ty.

Psalms 92:1-5
Enos 1:27

129 The Spirit of God

New Settings

William W. Phelps

Traditional Scottish Melody, arr. Brent Yorgason

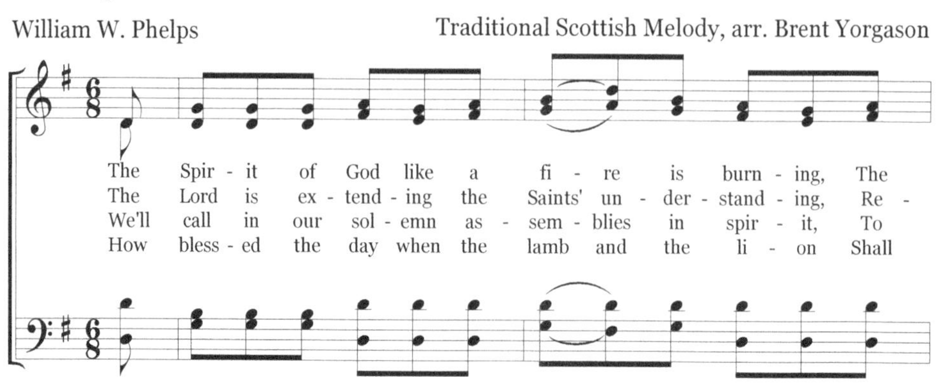
The Spir - it of God like a fi - re is burn - ing, The
The Lord is ex - tend - ing the Saints' un - der - stand - ing, Re -
We'll call in our sol - emn as - sem - blies in spir - it, To
How bless - ed the day when the lamb and the li - on Shall

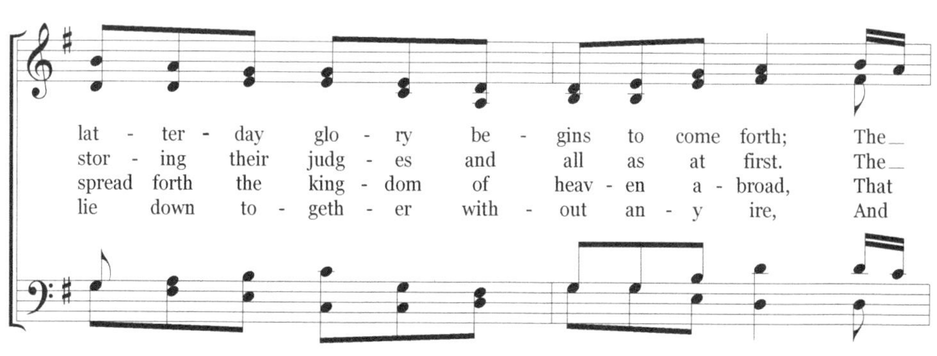
lat - ter - day glo - ry be - gins to come forth; The
stor - ing their judg - es and all as at first. The
spread forth the king - dom of heav - en a - broad, That
lie down to - geth - er with - out an - y ire, And

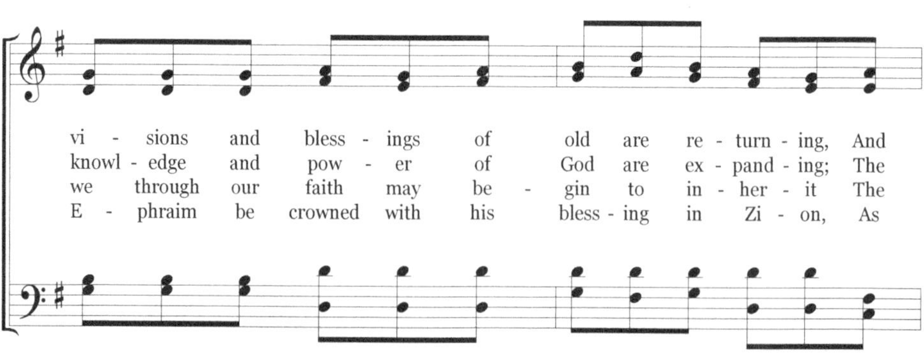
vi - sions and bless - ings of old are re - turn - ing, And
knowl - edge and pow - er of God are ex - pand - ing; The
we through our faith may be - gin to in - her - it The
E - phraim be crowned with his bless - ing in Zi - on, As

an - gels are com - ing to vis - it the earth. We'll
veil o'er the earth is be - gin - ning to burst.
vi - sions and bless - ings and glo - ries of God.
Je - sus de - scends in His char - iot of fire!
sing and we'll shout with the ar - mies of hea - ven, Ho -
san - na, ho - san - na to God and the Lamb! Let glo - ry to them in the
high - est be gi - ven, Hence - forth and for - ev - er, A - men and a - men!

Doctrine and Covenants 109:79-80
Doctrine and Covenants 100

130 When through the Deep Waters

New Settings

Robert Keen
Kevin G. Pace
When through the deep wa - ters I call thee to go, The
When through fi - ery tri - als thy path - way shall lie, My
E'en down to old age, all my peo - ple shall prove My
The soul that on Je - sus hath leaned for re - pose I
riv - ers of sor - row shall not thee o'er - flow, For
grace, all suf - fi - cient, shall be thy sup - ply. The
sov - 'reign e - ter - nal, un - change - a - ble love; And
will not, I can - not, de - sert to His foes; That
I will be with thee, thy trou - bles to bless, And
flame shall not hurt thee; I on - ly de - sign Thy
then, when gray hair shall their tem - ples a - dorn, Like
soul, though all hell should en - deav - or to shake, I'll
sanc - ti - fy to thee thy deep - est dis - tress.
dross to con - sume and thy gold to re - fine.
lambs shall they still in my bos - om be borne.
nev - er, no nev - er, no nev - er for - sake.

Alma 38:5

131
New Settings

Ye Elders of Israel

Cyrus H. Wheelock

John Roberts, arr. Brent Yorgason

Ye el - ders of Is - rael, come join now with me And seek out the righ - teous, wher - e'er they may be; In des - ert, on moun - tain, on land, or on sea; And bring them to Zi - on, the pure and the free.
The har - vest is great, and the la - b'rers are few; But if we're u - nit - ed, we all things can do. We'll gath - er the wheat from the midst of the tares And bring them from bond - age, from sor - rows and snares. O
We'll go to the poor, like our Cap - tain of old, And vis - it the wea - ry, the hun - gry, and cold; We'll cheer up their hearts with the news that He bore And point them to Zi - on and life ev - er - more.

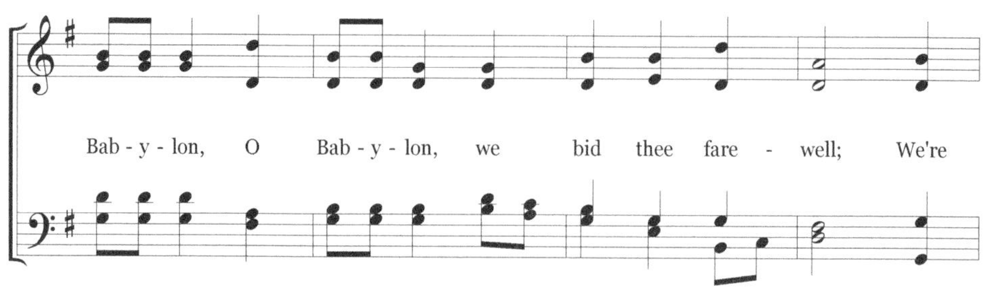
Bab - y - lon, O Bab - y - lon, we bid thee fare - well; We're

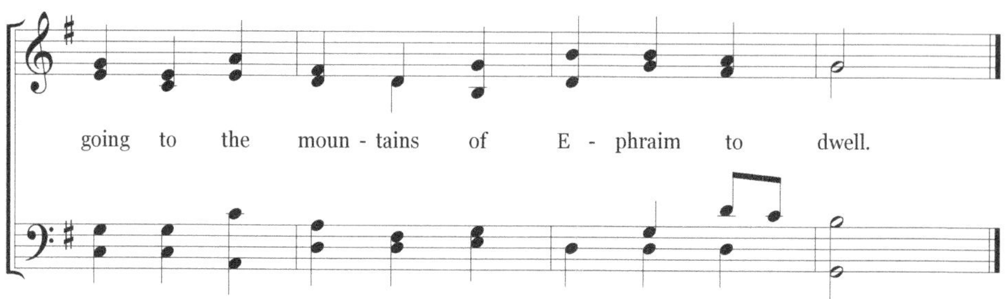
going to the moun - tains of E - phraim to dwell.

Doctrine and Covenants 133:7-9, 14
Doctrine and Covenants 75:2-5

A Cradle Hymn

Isaac Watts — Rick Graham

Hush! my dear, lie still and slum - ber, Ho - ly an - gels
Soft and ea - sy is thy cra - dle: Coarse and hard thy
See the kind - er shep - herds round Him, Tell - ing won - ders
How much bet - ter thou'rt at - tend - ed than the Son of
guard thy bed! Heav'n - ly bless - ings with - out num - ber
Sav - ior lay, When His birth - place was a sta - ble
from the sky! Where they sought Him, there they found Him,
God could be, when from heav - en He de - scend - ed
gent - ly fall - ing on thy head.
and His soft - est bed was hay.
With His vir - gin moth - er by.
and be - came a child like thee!

Luke 2:7

133 A Day Without Night

Christmas Hymns

Hillary Abplanalp

Hillary Abplanalp and Pamalee Mann

Lift up your head. Be of cheer. Be - hold the time is at hand. On this night the sign shall ap - pear of a king in a dis - tant land. He'll come un-to His own to ful - fill all He's made known. Look up to the light. Re - mem - ber this
Lift up your head. Be of cheer. Come lis - ten brave Ne - phite son. Far a - way a child lies a - sleep the On - ly Be - got - ten one. He'll come un-to His own to ful - fill all He's made known. Look up to the light. Re - mem - ber this
Lift up your head. Be of cheer. Be - hold the star in the sky. Now ful - filled the proph - e - cy of the child who was sent that night. He'll come un-to His own to ful - fill all He's made known. Be - lieve, don't you cry. Now we will not

night. For this is the day the Lord is born.
night. For this is the day the Lord is born.
die, For this is the day the Lord is born.
At the set - ting of the sun there was no dark - ness.
A
Ah - - - - - - He'll come un-to His
new star ap - peared. The wick - ed fell to earth.
own to ful - fill all He's made known. Look up to the light. Re -
mem - ber this night. For this is the day the Lord is born.

3 Nephi 1:15-16

134

Blessed Baby, Savior of Men

Christmas Hymns

Gary Croxall

Kathleen Holyoak

God has come to save all men and rests a ba - by in
Ma - ry holds the lit - tle King, who wears no crown, who
Un - der a sky where shines His light, He nods and there is

Beth - le - hem. An - gels have gath - ered up a - bove to
has no ring. Soft is the lu - la - by she speaks, for
si - lent night. Where the ox and lamb have fed, Christ

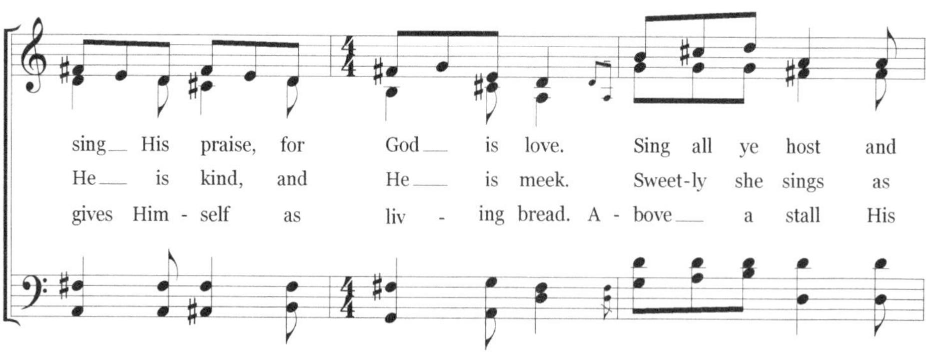
sing His praise, for God is love. Sing all ye host and
He is kind, and He is meek. Sweet-ly she sings as
gives Him - self as liv - ing bread. A - bove a stall His

speak His name, for Christ the Lord shall rule and reign.
she at - tends, the bless - ed ba - by, Sav-ior of men.
star doth shine, hail-ing the Son of God di - vine.

Luke 2:12

Christmas Star

Anonymous

Rick Graham

A dia - mond shines no bright - er than that love - ly Christ - mas star. It shines in all it's bril - liance it's seen from near or far.
A sym - bol of the Christ child as He lay up - on the hay, It tells to all the wait - ing world a King was born that day.
Give us strength and hope and cour - age to do our best by far And nev - er fal - ter in our faith as we watch that Christ - mas star.
O Beth - le - hem Star keep shin - ing. Give us faith and hope and

love. Keep our thoughts for-ev - er turn-ing to the Sav - ior up a - bove.

Helaman 14:5
3 Nephi 1:21

Glory Hallelujah!

Norma Boyd

Norma Boyd

Hark! Hark! Her - ald an - gels sing - ing. Hark! Hark!
Ma - ry lays Him in a man - ger. Jo - seph
In the sky a star is gleam - ing. Hope and
Hark! Hark! Christ - mas bells are ring - ing. Hark! Hark!

Joy - ous news they're bring - ing. "Je - sus is born in
guards Him from all dan - ger. Wise men will come and
light are from it stream - ing. It tells the world a
Glad the song they're sing - ing. "Je - sus is born in

Beth - le - hem, Ju - de - a. Je - sus is born! Sing
hum - bly kneel be - fore Him. Shep - herds are say - ing,
great - er light is dawn - ing. Je - sus is born this
Beth - le - hem, Ju - de - a! Je - sus is born! Sing

glo - ry Hal - le - lu - jah!"
"Come, let us a - dore Him!"
joy - ous Christ - mas morn - ing.
glo - ry Hal - le - lu - jah!"

Luke 2:14

137 Holy Was That Wondrous Night

Christmas Hymns

Hyrum Mead

Rosemary Mead

Reverently (♩.=48)
1. Ho - ly was that won - drous night, When the heav - ens o - pened bright,
2. Ho - ly was his hum - ble birth, In a sta - ble born on earth.
3. Ho - ly is the Prince of Peace, He whose won - ders nev - er cease,
And de - scend - ed Di - vine Love, God's own Son sent from a - bove,
'Midst the cat - tle and the lambs, Meek - ly slept the great I Am.
Whose de scent be - low us all Van - quished death and Ad - am's fall,
Marked in com - ing by a star, Seen by wise men from a - far.
He who count - less worlds had made In a man - ger's straw was laid.
He came on that ho - ly night To turn dark - ness in - to light.

Luke 2:13-14

138 How Precious the Hope

Christmas Hymns

Michael D. Young

Flemish Carol, arr. Michael D. Young

How pre - cious the hope that we all now en - joy be - cause of the first Christ - mas night.
How pre - cious the fruit that the seed of faith bears as we seek our Sav - ior to - day.
How bril - liant the dawn of that glo - ri - ous morn when next He re - turns to the earth.
How last - ing the peace that we all now can claim be - cause of His bright, heal - ing light.
As the bright new star led the wise men a - long the Spir - it now shows us the way.
Re - turn - ing in splen - dor as Sav - ior and King, and not as His once hum - ble birth.
Oh, let us sing out with the an - gels, who first brought the news of His birth. Whose

voic - es still ech - o through a - ges, "Bring peace to all men on earth!"

Moroni 7:42
Romans 15:13

I Am the Light

Michelle Witte
Michelle Witte
I am the light that shin - eth forth in dark - ness.
Sweet is the light that leads all souls to good - ness.
Re - ceive my light, the glo - ry of my gos - pel.
Light com - pre - hend - eth all: large (and) small in God's king - dom.
God, in His heav'n a - bove, by (his) love sends it to thee.
Bring truth in - to (thy) mind, seek (and) find love and learn - ing.
Dis cern the truth- (by) me, Look un - - to my - lan - tern.
Know that His light (will) dwell with the meek and low - ly,
Let thy light (so) shine un - to all thy breth - ren;
1,2
3
Ev - er I will shine, with - out end.
Ev - er shin - ing on with - out end.
Ev - er let it burn with - out end.

Doctrine and Covenants 34:2
Mosiah 16:9

In Bethlehem There Lies a King

Gary Croxall

Kathleen Holyoak

I found Him in a man - ger where I
A won - drous child in swad - dling clothes, A
In Beth - le - hem there lies a King. "Be
I saw the an - gel of the Lord whose
The shep - herds came and wise men too. They
In Beth - le - hem there lies a King. "Be -
touched His hand and smoothed His hair, He smiled at me and
blos - som fair - er than a rose. In Beth - le - hem I
hold His star," the_ an - gels sing. "The Lord of lords is
voice did pierce me_ to the core. "Fear not," he spoke with
knelt be - fore this ba - by, who Was born to rule as
hold His star," the_ an - gels sing. "The Lord of lords is
I felt peace while in a sta - ble filled with beasts.
found the babe and heard the an - gels sing His praise.
born this day and rests up - on a bed of hay."
sol - emn word, "For this is Je - sus Christ, the Lord."
King of kings and take a - way our cares and sins.
born this day and rests up - on a bed of hay."

Luke 2:7

141 In David's Lowly City

Christmas Hymns

Peter Gates | Peter Gates

In Da - vid's low - ly ci - ty A wea - ry ba - by lay. The
His mo - ther rocks Him soft - ly And sings Him lul - la - bies. The
Oh, sleep my lit - tle Sav - ior! Sleep, my heav'n - ly light! To -
Lord of all is sleep - ing; He wears a crown of hay. The
an - gel hosts stand si - lent With won - der in their eyes. The
mor - row comes the morn - ing. Now sleep on through the night. To -
Lord of all is sleep - ing; He wears a crown of hay.
an - gel hosts stand si - lent With-won - der in their eyes.
mor - row comes the morn - ing. Now sleep on through the
1,2
3
night. Sleep, sleep, Oh, sleep.

Luke 2

Let the Earth and Angels Sing

Hyrum Mead
Rosemary Mead
Let the earth and an - gels sing Prais - es to the new-born King.
Let the proph - ets who fore-told Of His birth, with joy be - hold.
Let the wise men, near and far, Seek and find His guid - ing star.
Let them lift their voic - es high, Shout ho - san - nas 'cross the sky!
Long they wait - ed for the time Of His ho - ly birth di - vine.
'Cross the earth and through the night, Lead them with a ho - ly light,
All cre - a - tion, rise and say, "Christ the Lord is born this day!"
They fore-saw this glo - rious morn, The Re - deem - er, Christ, is born!
Till at last His face they'll see, Wor - ship - ing on bend - ed knee!

Luke 2:13-14

143 Little Lamb

Christmas Hymns

Rick Graham — Rick Graham

Lit-tle lamb in man-ger stall, ox and sheep in si-lence awed. We be-hold His ten-der face, Je-sus, Sav-ior of the hu-man race.
Lit-tle lamb, Thy birth fore-told from Thy ser-vants young and old. Proph-e-sied from a-ges past now ful-filled our Sav-ior comes at last.
Lit-tle lamb, oh bless-ed One! Thou are God's be-got-ten Son. Born to Ma-ry, vir-gin mild. God in-car-nate and born mor-tal child.
Lit-tle lamb, ful-fill the plan, back with Fa-ther it be-gan when we heard these words di-vine: "Send me, and the glo-ry all be Thine!
Lit-tle lamb, our joy, our all! May our hearts re-ceive the call. Loud ho-san-nas, let us sing to our Lord, and lamb, E-ter-nal King!

Luke 2:15-16

My Heart Will Always Linger

Michael Young, J.C. Aaberg

Danish Carol arr. Michael D. Young

My heart will al - ways lin - ger with - in the ho - ly room. Where
Oh, come and I will o - pen, my lov - ing heart and mind, To
Oh, come let me en - fold you, with love too great to speak, As
first our ho - ly Mas - ter dis - pelled the wor - ld's gloom. My
be your hum - ble dwell - ing. Oh, come and sweet - ly find A
once your mo - ther wrapped you when you were small and meek. And
faith finds there its trea - sure, My soul, its pure de - light, Its
place where you might en - ter, A place to lay your head. As
may your light shine o'er me, That all may see a - far, The
joy be - yond all mea - sure, The Lord of Christ-mas night.
on that bless - ed Christ - mas, You found a man - ger bed.
glo - ry of your pres ence, As shone your Christ-mas star.

Luke 2:15-16

145

Christmas Hymns

Sing Hallelujah!

Norma Boyd

Norma Boyd

Born in a low - ly sta - ble in Beth - le - hem,
An - gels sang songs of joy at Je - sus's birth,
Shep - herds be - lieved the words the an - gels pro - claimed.
Je - sus, the new - born babe, in man - ger He lay.

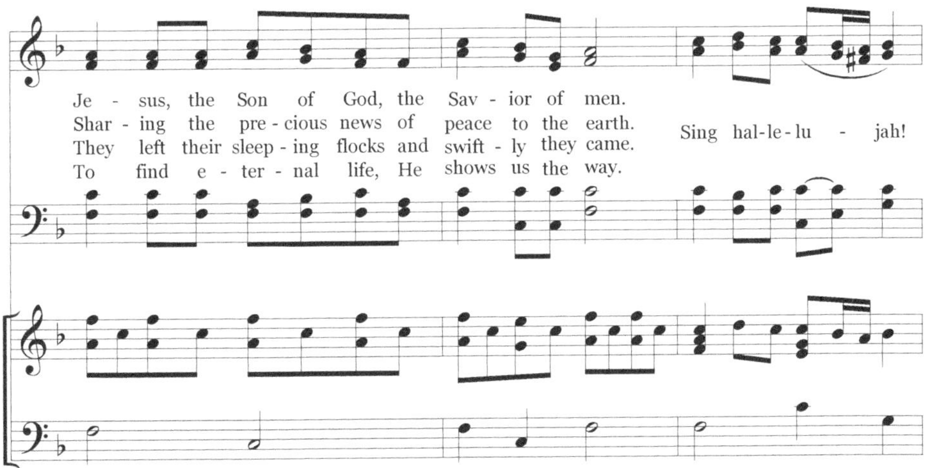

Je - sus, the Son of God, the Sav - ior of men.
Shar - ing the pre - cious news of peace to the earth.
They left their sleep - ing flocks and swift - ly they came.
To find e - ter - nal life, He shows us the way.
Sing hal - le - lu - jah!

Sing hal-le-lu - jah! Sing hal-le-lu - jah! Je-sus is born!
Je - sus is born! Sing hal - le - lu - jah! Sing hal - le - lu - jah!
Sing hal - le - lu - jah! Je - sus is born!
rit.

Luke 2:15-16

146

The City of David

Gary Croxall

Kathleen Holyoak

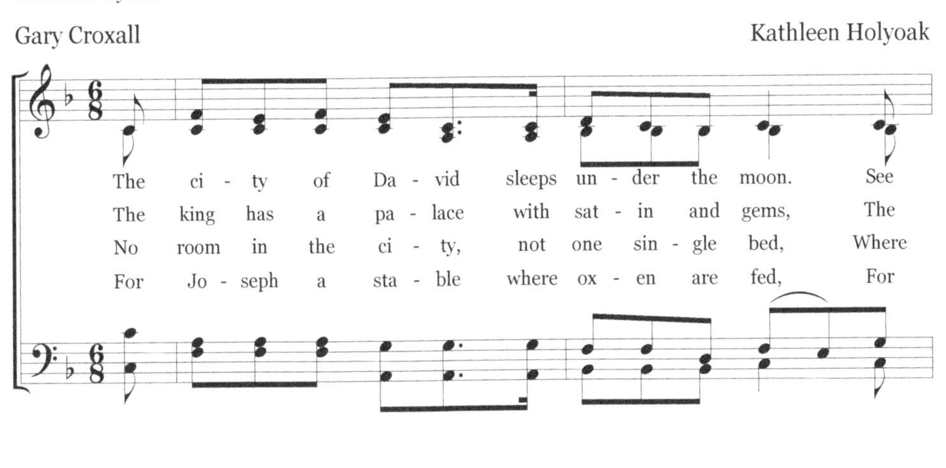
The ci - ty of Da - vid sleeps un - der the moon. See
The king has a pa - lace with sat - in and gems, The
No room in the ci - ty, not one sin - gle bed, Where
For Jo - seph a sta - ble where ox - en are fed, For

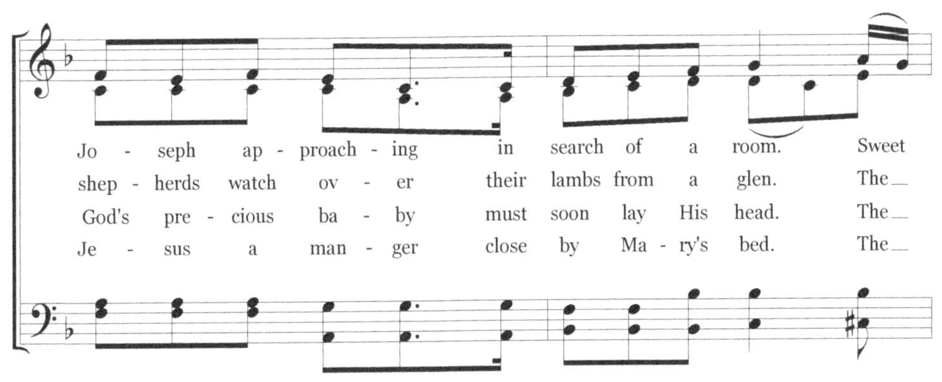
Jo - seph ap - proach - ing in search of a room. Sweet
shep - herds watch ov - er their lambs from a glen. The
God's pre - cious ba - by must soon lay His head. The
Je - sus a man - ger close by Ma - ry's bed. The

Ma - ry's be - side him, her time draw - ing nigh, But
wise men shall sleep in their tents grand and rare, But
Sav - ior is com - ing on this night of nights, But
King of Cre - a - tion, who comes to a - tone, Shall

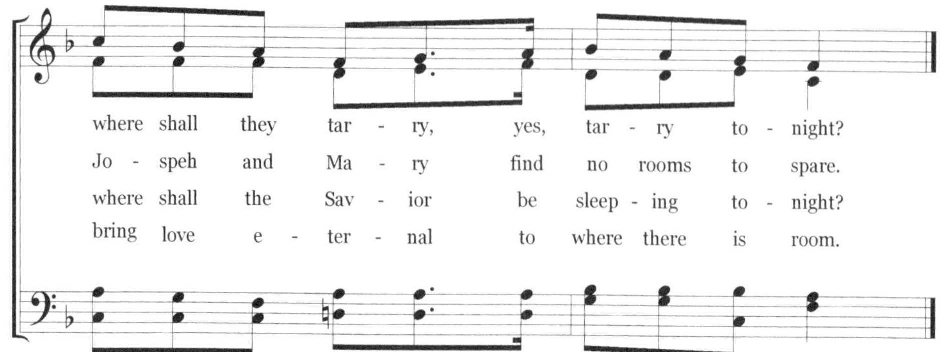
where shall they tar - ry, yes, tar - ry to - night?
Jo - speh and Ma - ry find no rooms to spare.
where shall the Sav - ior be sleep - ing to - night?
bring love e - ter - nal to where there is room.

Luke 2:4

147
Christmas Hymns

The Night Was Still

Gary Croxall
Kathleen Holyoak
The night was still when from a-bove, sweet
They came in haste to Beth-le-hem and
mu-sic soft-ly fell. As an-gels sang a song of joy to
found with-in a stall Good Jo-seph with Ma-ry, who knelt be-side a
shep-herds on a hill.
ba-by so pure and small.
"For un-to you a Sav-ior is born, and
He is Christ the Lord. "Peace on earth, good will to men," the won-d'ring shep-herds
1
2
heard. heard.
A

babe like no oth-er, a mo-ther so mild, God's light stream-ing down from a - bove. The
an-gels from heav-en in joy-ous re-frain all prais-ing the heav-en-sent child. For
un - to you a Sav - ior is born, and He is Christ the
Lord. "Peace on earth, good will to men," the won - d'ring shep - herds,
rall.
won - d'ring shep - herds heard. "Peace on earth, good will to men."

Luke 2

148 Away in a Manger

New Christmas Settings

Traditional English Carol — Traditional German Hymn, arr. Michael D. Young

A - way in a man - ger, no crib for His bed, The
The cat - tle are low - ing, the poor ba - by wakes; But
Be near me, Lord Je - sus; I ask Thee to stay Close
O Beau - ti - ful Sav - vior, Lord of the na - tions.
lit - tle Lord Je - sus laid down His sweet head; The
lit - tle Lord Je - sus, no cry - ing He makes. I
by me for - ev - er and love me, I pray. Bless
Son of God and Son of Man.
stars in the heav - ens looked down where He lay, The
love Thee, Lord Je - sus, look down from the sky And
all the dear child - ren in Thy ten - der care, And
Thee will I hon - or, praise, and give glo - ry, Give
lit - tle Lord Je - sus a - sleep on the hay.
stay by my cra - dle till morn - ing is nigh.
fit us for hea - ven to live with there.
praise and glo - ry ev - er - more.

Luke 2:7
Luke 18:15-17

149 I Heard the Bells on Christmas Day

New Christmas Settings

William Wadsworth Longfellow

Traditional Spiritual, arr. Michael D. Young

I heard the bells on Christ-mas day their old fa - mil - iar car - ols
And in de - spair I bowed my head: "There is no peace on earth," I
Till ring - ing, sing - ing on its way the world re-volved from night to
play, And wild and sweet the words re - peat of peace on earth, good will to
said. "For hate is strong and mocks the song of peace on earth, good will to
day, A voice, a chime, a chant sub-lime, of peace on earth, good will to
men. I thought how, as the day had come, the bel - fries of all Chris - ten -
men." Then pealed the bells more loud and deep."God is not dead, nor doth He
men. And ev - ery year I hear them still. Their soar - ing song my soul does
dom Had rolled a - long, th'un-bro-ken song of peace on earth, good will to men.
sleep; The wrong shall fail, the right pre-vail with peace on earth, good will to men."
fill With ho - ly peace, and I in - crease in peace on earth, good will to men.

Luke 2:14
Doctrine and Covenants 3:1-3

150 It Came upon the Midnight Clear

New Christmas Settings

Edmund H. Sears | American Folk Song, arr. Michael D. Young

It came up - pon the mid - night clear, that glo - rious song of old, From
Still thru the clo - ven skies they come with peace - ful wings un - furled, And
For lo! The days are has - t'ning on, by prop - hets seen of old, When
an - gels bend - ing near the earth to touch their harps of gold. Peace
still their heav'n - ly mu - sic floats o'er all the wea - ry world. A -
with the ev - er - cir - cling years shall come the time fore - told, When
on the earth, good will to men from heav'n's all - gra - cious King. The
bove its sad and low - ly plains, they bend on hov - 'ring wing. And
the new heav'n and earth shall own the Prince of Peace their King, And
world in sol - emn still - ness lay to hear the an - gels sing.
ev - er o'er its ba - bel sounds the bless - ed an - gels sing.
the whole world send back the song which now the an - gels sing.
Ah

Luke 2:8-17
Alma 5:50

151 O Come, All Ye Faithful

New Christmas Settings

John F. Wade

Ludwig Van Beethoven arr. Michael D. Young

O come, all ye faith - ful, joy - ful and tri - ump - phant, O
Sing, ye choirs of an - gels, Sing in ex - ul - ta - tion! O
Yea, Lord, we all greet Thee, born this hap - py morn - ing. O
come ye, O come ye, O come ye to Beth - le - hem. Come be - hold Him,
sing, ye, O sing, ye, O sing, ye in heav'n a - bove. Glo - ry, glo - ry,
Je - sus, to Thee, be Un - to Thee all glo - ry giv'n. Son of Fa - ther,
Come be - hold Him, born the King of an - gels.
glo - ry to God, glo - ry to God, the high - est.
Son of the Fa - ther, Now in flesh ap - pear - ing.
O come, let us a - dore Him, Come a - dore Him, Christ, the Lord!

Luke 2:8-20
Psalm 95:6

152

O Holy Night

New Christmas Settings

John Sullivan Dwight — Michael D. Young

O ho - ly night, the stars are bright - ly shin - ing. It is the night of our dear Sav - ior's birth. Long lay the world in sin and er - ror pin - ing, Till He ap - peared and the soul felt its worth. A thrill of hope; the wea - ry world re - joic - es, For
Led by the light of faith se - rene - ly beam - ing, With glow - ing hearts by His cra - dle we stand. Now o'er the world a star is sweet - ly stream - ing Now come wise men from out of O - rient land. The King of kings lay thus in low - ly man - ger, In
Tru - ly He taught us to love one a - noth - er. His law is love and His gos - pel is peace. Chains shall He break for the slave is our broth - er, And in His name all op - pres - sion shall cease. Sweet hymns of joy in grate - ful chor - us raise we. Let

yon-der breaks a new and glo-rious morn. Oh, fall on your
all our trials born to be our friend. Oh, He knows our
all with-in us praise His ho-ly name. Oh, Christ is the
knees, oh, hear the an-gel voic-es. O night di-vine, O
need, our weak-ness, He's no strang-er. Be-hold your King. Be-
Lord, for-e-ver, e-ver praise we, His pow-er and glo-ry
night, when Christ was born. O night di-vine. O night di-vine. O
fore Him low-ly bend. Be-hold your King! Be-hold your King. Be-
ev-er more pro-claim. His pow'r and glo-ry more pro-claim. E'er
night di-vine!
hold your King!
more pro-claim!
Ho-ly night di-vine!
Oh, be-hold your King!
Ev-er more pro-claim!

Luke 2

153

Silent Night

New Christmas Settings

Franz Gruber

Folk Song, arr. Michael D. Young

Si - lent night! Ho - ly night! All is calm, all is bright
Si - lent night, ho - ly night, Shep - herds quake at the sight.
Si - lent night, ho - ly night, Son of God, love's true light.
Round yon vir - gin, moth - er and child, Ho - ly in-fant, so ten - der and mild.
Glo - ries stream from heav - en a - far, heav'n - ly hosts sing hal - le - lu - jah!
Ra - diant beams from Thy ho - ly face, with the dawn of re - deem - ing grace.
Sleep in heav - en, heav'n - ly peace, Sleep in heav'n - ly peace.
Christ, the Sav - ior, He is born. Christ, the Sav-ior, He is born!
Je - sus, Lord, at Thy birth. Je - sus,Lord, at Thy birth.
Si - lent night! Ho - ly night! All is calm, all is bright.

Luke 2:7-14
Alma 7:10-12

154 With Wondering Awe

New Christmas Settings

Anon.

Gabriel Faure, arr. Michael D. Young

With won - d'ring awe the wise men saw The
By light of star they trav - eled far To
And still is found, the world a - round, The
The heav'n - ly star its rays a - far On
star in heav - en spring - ing, And with de - light in
seek the low - ly man - ger, A hum - ble bed where-
old and hal - lowed sto - ry, And still is sung in
ev - 'ry land is throw - ing, And shall not cease till
peace - ful night, They heard the an - gels sing - ing.
in was laid The won - drous lit - tle strang - er.
ev - 'ry tongue The an - gels' song of glor - y.
ho - ly peace In all the earth is grow - ing.

Ho - san - na, ho - san - na, ho - san - na to His name.
1, 2, 3
Ho - san - na, ho - san - na, ho - san - na to His name!
4.
name!
4.

Matthew 2:1-11

155

Easter Hymns

Early That Morn

Rick Graham

Rick Graham

Ear - ly that morn, the Sab - bath done, the wom - en come, e're
With heav - y heart, they on - ward tread 'neath skies of pur - ple,
As they ar - rived, to their sur - prise the stone was rolled, their
And at the en - trance of the tomb, an an - gel then dis -
He Lives! My Sav - ior, Lord, and King! Let heav'n and earth, His
ris - ing sun. With spic - es lad - en by death's hill
blue, and red. With - in that sep - ul - chre was lain,
voic - es cried, "The emp - ty tomb! To where? We pray,
pelled their gloom. "Why seek the liv - ing from the dead?
prais - es sing! For He ful - filled His Fa - ther's plan,
now press - ing through the gar - den still.
their pre - cious Je - sus, who was slain.
for they have tak - en Him a - way!"
For He has ris - en, as He said!"
to bring to pass im - mor - tal man!

Luke 23: 53-56
Luke 24:1-9

156 He Walked Alone So We Must Not

Easter Hymns

Michael D. Young

Rick Graham

He walked a - lone so we must not, a -
A lone - ly road all choked with thorns, that
There was no one to walk be - side as
Tell of His grace, lest we for - get the

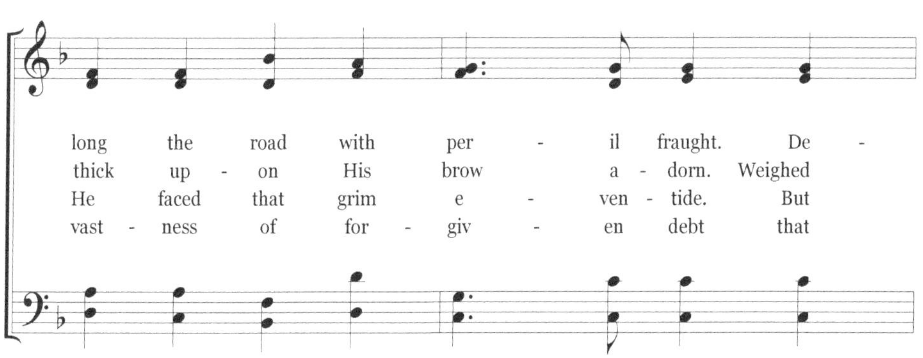

long the road with per - il fraught. De -
thick up - on His brow a - dorn. Weighed
He faced that grim e - ven - tide. But
vast - ness of for - giv - en debt that

scend - ing to the dark - est vale, the
down by bur - dens stark and grave, great
glo - ry to our God as - cribe, He
ran - soms ev - 'ry mor - tal child, and

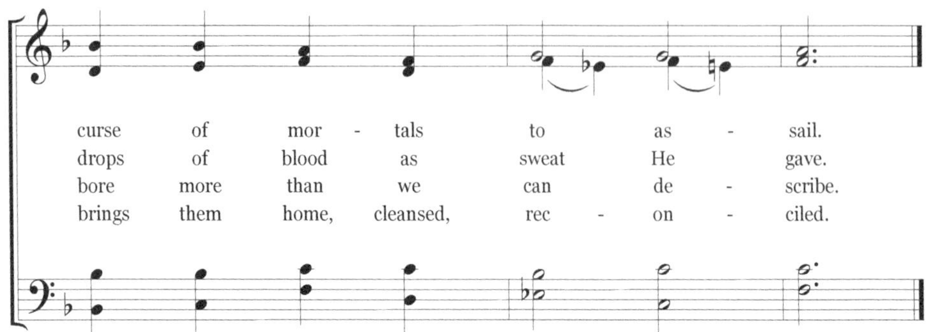
curse of mor - tals to as - sail.
drops of blood as sweat He gave.
bore more than we can de - scribe.
brings them home, cleansed, rec - on - ciled.

John 16:32

157
Easter Hymns

On Easter Morn

Hyrum Mead

Rosemary Mead

On Eas - ter morn we come re - joic - ing In our Lord, who rose this day, Who bore the bur - den of our sin, The sting of death to take a - way.
T'was Eas - ter morn when Ma - ry met Him, Un - as - cend - ed, yet with love He paused to turn her grief to joy Be - fore He rose to rule a - bove.
Oh, may this world of tears and sor - row, Filled with grief and death and pain, Find hope, for Je - sus, Lord tri - um - phant Bore our grief and rose a - gain!
On Eas - ter morn we come re - joic - ing, For the stone is rolled a - way! The tomb is emp - ty and the Christ our King and Sav - ior is ris'n this day!

Mosiah 16:8
1 Corinthians 15:55

158

Resurrection Hymn

Easter Hymns

Nathan Howe

Nathan Howe

A man of sor-rows, Je - sus came To con - quer sin and death for man,
In the be - gin - ning was the Word, The Christ who made the earth and sky.
And when in sor - row, we in prayer Ap - proach the Fa - ther will - ling - ly,
That by the pow - er of His name We might ful - fill the Fa - ther's plan.
The Fa-ther's po - wer was con - ferred That He should live and choose to die.
To o - ver - come temp - ta - tion's snare Or to en - dure ad - ver - si - ty,
Though He has drunk our bit - ter cup, And for our sake His blood was shed,
He com - pre - hend - ed ev - ery pain, Knew ev - ery weak - ness, ev - ery sin,
The Ho - ly Ghost can heal our souls, For the A - tone - ment paid the price.

He is not here, but ris - en up; Seek not the li - ving with the dead!
For on - ly He could break the chains And bring the cap - tives home a - gain.
The Sav-ior came to make us whole: O come, re - cieve the liv - ing Christ!
He was lift - ed on the cross That He might lift us to the Fa - ther; He has
He was lift - ed on the cross That He might lift us to the Fa - ther; He has
Ho - san - na to the Lamb, Who is the first-fruits of the Fa - ther! He will
ris - en from the tomb That through Him we so may rise.
ris - en from the tomb That through Him we so may rise.
come a - gain to reign, And through Him we all shall rise.

Mosiah 15:20-26

159 Bearers of God's Holy Priesthood

Priesthood Hymns

Michael D. Young

Rick Graham

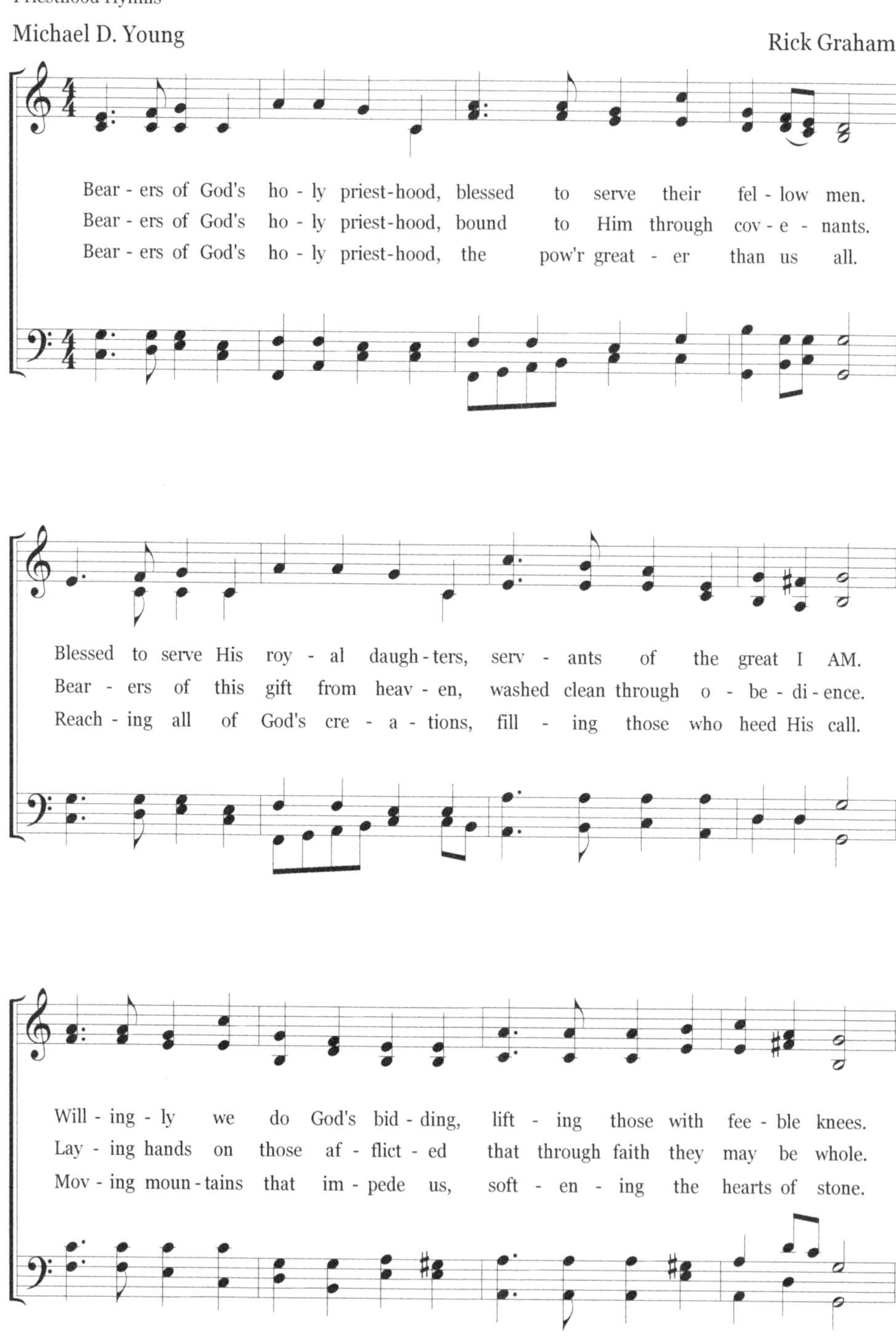
Bear - ers of God's ho - ly priest-hood, blessed to serve their fel - low men.
Bear - ers of God's ho - ly priest-hood, bound to Him through cov - e - nants.
Bear - ers of God's ho - ly priest-hood, the pow'r great - er than us all.
Blessed to serve His roy - al daugh - ters, serv - ants of the great I AM.
Bear - ers of this gift from heav - en, washed clean through o - be - di - ence.
Reach - ing all of God's cre - a - tions, fill - ing those who heed His call.
Will - ing - ly we do God's bid - ding, lift - ing those with fee - ble knees.
Lay - ing hands on those af - flict - ed that through faith they may be whole.
Mov - ing moun - tains that im - pede us, soft - en - ing the hearts of stone.

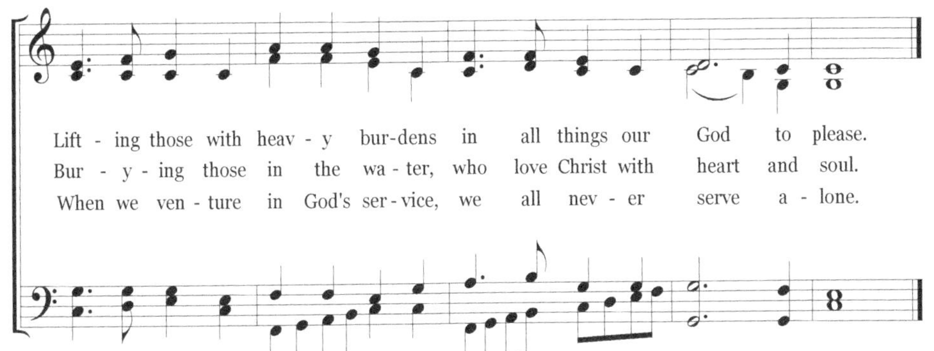
Lift - ing those with heav - y bur-dens in all things our God to please.
Bur - y - ing those in the wa - ter, who love Christ with heart and soul.
When we ven - ture in God's ser - vice, we all nev - er serve a - lone.

Doctrine and Covenants 124:123
Doctrine and Covenants 107:40

160 Charity, Never Failing

Relief Society Hymns

Toni Thomas

Annette Dickman

Char-i-ty is pure love, The song of a wom-an's heart. It
Char-i-ty is serv-ing Our Sav-ior who dwells a-bove By
Char-i-ty is bound-less When set-tled un-to the soul. It

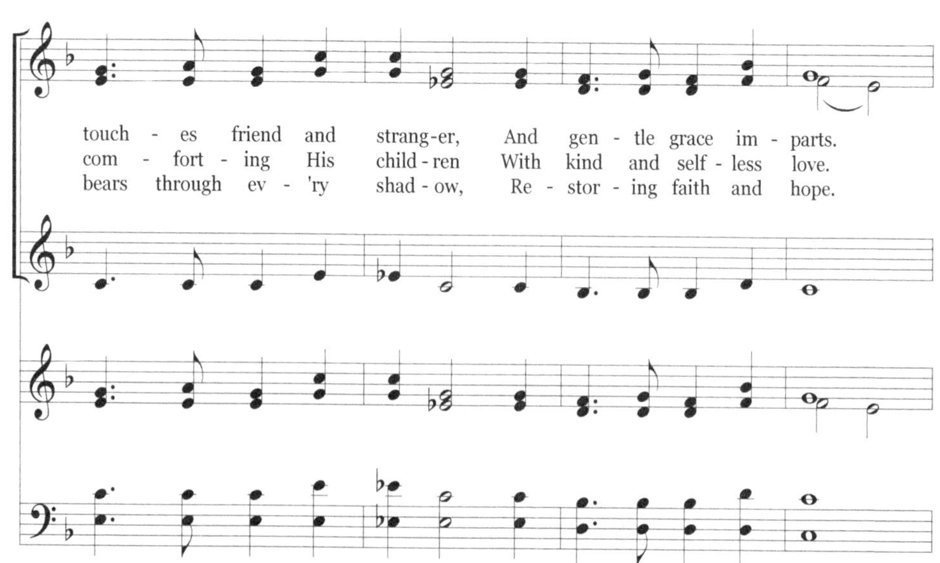
touch-es friend and strang-er, And gen-tle grace im-parts.
com-fort-ing His child-ren With kind and self-less love.
bears through ev-'ry shad-ow, Re-stor-ing faith and hope.

Love pu - ri - fies our pur - pose And tem - pers way - ward thought: With
Christ lov - ing us com - plete - ly, Our sins and sor - rows bought: With
Time takes a - way all trea - sure Of fleet - ing worth or flawed: With

char-i - ty nev - er fail - ing, We be - come as one with God.
char-i - ty nev - er fail - ing, We re - turn our thanks to God.
char-i - ty nev - er fail - ing, ap - proach the throne of God.

Moroni 7:46

161 Daughters in His Kingdom

Relief Society Hymns

Esther Megargel
Esther Megargel
We are daugh - ters in His king - dom, Who seek to serve the
As we lay a - side our world - ly cares, And seek for things a -
As we sing the songs of righ - teous - ness, Our prayers to God are
Lord. If we are faith - ful to the end, We'll gain a great re -
bove, We will speak forth our kind - est words, In tones of pur - est
said. He an - swers us by giv - ing forth A bless - ing on our
ward. We are teach - ers of our fam - i - lies, Our words we will im -
love. As we reach out to our neigh - bors, And help them feel their
heads. As our spir - its shine in meek - ness, With hum - ble, Christ - like
part, As we ex - pound the gos - pel truths From the wis - dom of our hearts.
worth, We bring com - fort to the wound - ed heart, As we serve as sis - ters on earth.
love. He will crown us with His righ - teous - ness. We will dwell with God a - bove.

Doctrine and Covenants 25

162 God's Infinite, Eternal Power

Priesthood Hymns

Michael D. Young

Rick Graham

The ves - sel is not great - er than the oil that lies with - in it. The
God's ser - vants fill their lamps a - new through His e - ter - nal grac - es. The
Then wor - thy ves - sels we must be and ser - vants pure and read - y. And
fire is so much bright - er than the spark that does be - gin it. The
Spir - it's fire kin - dled a - new where- e'er His smil - ing face is. The
hum - ble, prayer - ful we must be on roll - ing waves or stead - y. So
sun - light does not come from him who draws back each dark cur - tain, Nor
sun - light they al - low to shine to all those now dis - tres - sing. The
when God calls we, too may rise, ac - cept His heav'n - ly pow - er, For
does the moon shine on its own but shows the sun for
great - er light re - flect - ing to all those who seek God's
when the bride - groom comes a - gain, we know not when the

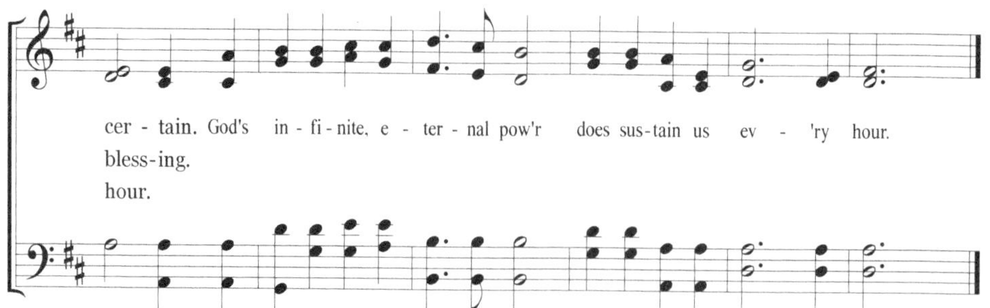
cer - tain. God's in - fi - nite, e - ter - nal pow'r does sus-tain us ev - 'ry hour.
bless-ing.
hour.

Doctrine and Covenants 20:28
Alma 34:10, 14

163 I Am Naught without My Savior

Priesthood Hymns

David Macfarlane | Nathan Howe

I am naught with - out my Sav - ior; I shall live to give Him laud.
In the days of my first les - sons, I was known to Him by name,
Send me, Lord, and I shall serve Thee; all my heart I give to Thee,
O Lord, I have trust - ed in Thee; I will trust in Thee for - e'er.
Taste of mer - cy I shall sa - vor as I grow to know my God.
Cho - sen by di - vine e - lec - tion ere the heav'n and earth were framed.
E'en my will sur - ren - dered to Thee, giv'n in all hu - mil - i - ty.
In the arm of flesh un - wor - thy is there glo - ry? No, not e'er.
Life e - ter - nal is Thy prom - ised life with Thee is my de - sire.
Walk - ing in His light, He taught me; Him I fol - lowed ev - 'ry hour.
Then, O rock of my sal - va - tion, guide me with Thy gen - tle hand.
E'er as - cends my voice in prais - es un - to Thee, my i - ron rod.

John 15:4-5

164 Live Up to Your Priviledge

Relief Society Hymns

Brooke C. Snow

Brook C. Snow

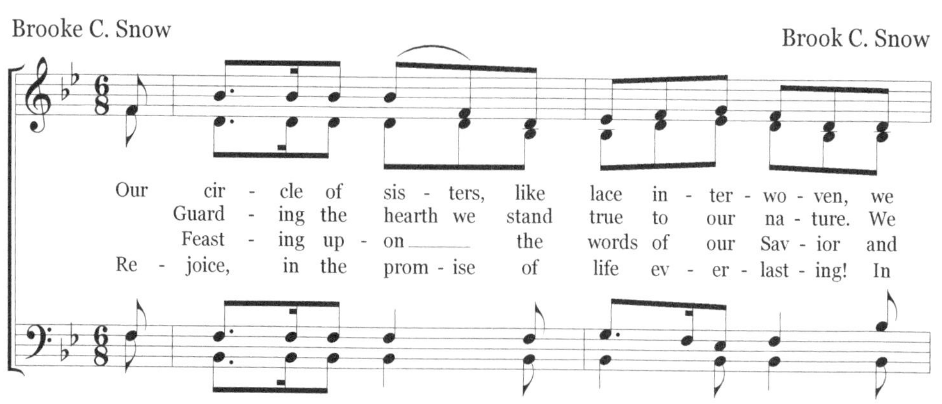
Our cir - cle of sis - ters, like lace in - ter - wo - ven, we
Guard - ing the hearth we stand true to our na - ture. We
Feast - ing up - on the words of our Sav - ior and
Re - joice, in the prom - ise of life ev - er - last - ing! In

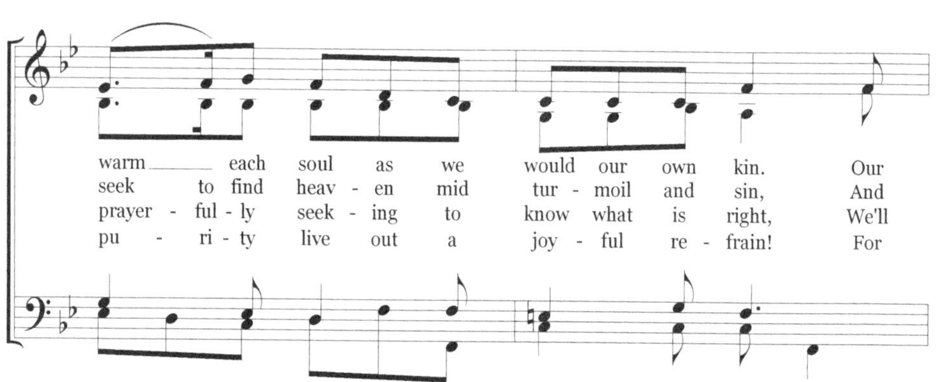
warm each soul as we would our own kin. Our
seek to find heav - en mid tur - moil and sin, And
prayer - ful - ly seek - ing to know what is right, We'll
pu - ri - ty live out a joy - ful re - frain! For

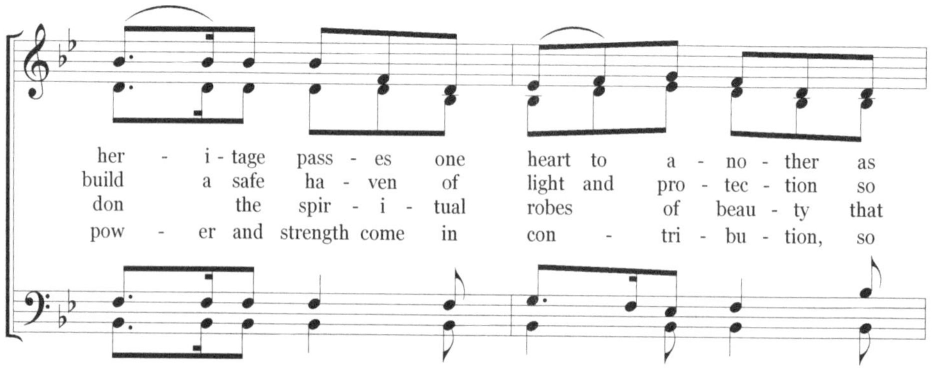
her - i - tage pass - es one heart to a - no - ther as
build a safe ha - ven of light and pro - tec - tion so
don the spir - i - tual robes of beau - ty that
pow - er and strength come in con - tri - bu - tion, so

char - i - ty fires the soul from with - in.
all may reach their po - ten - tial with - in. Live
come as a gift when we seek for the light.
walk with the Lord and with Him you will reign!

up to your priv'-lege, oh daugh-ters of Zi-on! For ours is a call-ing both no-ble and true! The

sav-ing of souls is a work and a bless-ing Where an-gels as-sist us in all that we do!

Articles of Faith 1:11
Titus 2:14

165 Priesthood Blessings

Priesthood Hymns

Kevin G. Pace
Kevin G. Pace
Gen - tle hands are placed up - on my head, and a
Priest - hood bless - ings are a sa - cred gift, giv'n to
An in - spir - ed state - ment from my God, wit - ness
Bless - ings tes - tif - y of God's great care, and of
bless - ing is con - ferred Through pro - phet - ic gift by a
ed - i - fy and con - sole, I do feel God's in - fin - ite
of the truths I seek, When I pass through sick - ness, ad -
Christ's div - in - i - ty, Giv'n as per - sonal rev - e -
ser - vant of God; I am blessed through priest - hood pow'r. How my
love o - ver me; I am lift - ed and re - newed. All my
ver - si - ty, I am strength - end by His word, Need - ed
la - tion to me if I'm wor - thy to re - ceive. As I

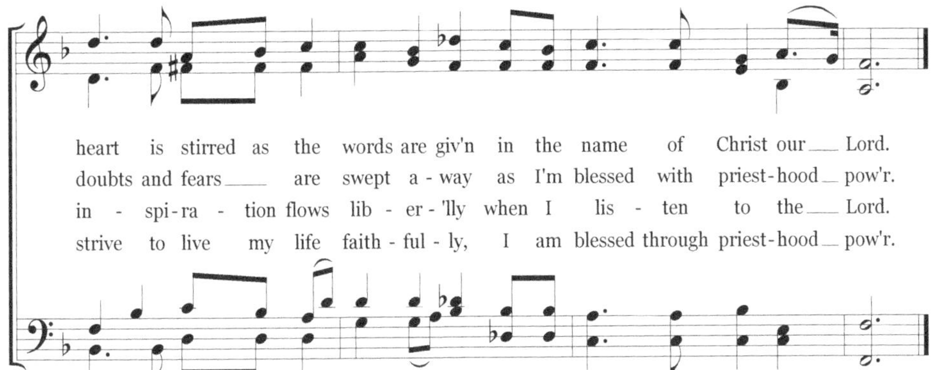
heart is stirred as the words are giv'n in the name of Christ our — Lord.
doubts and fears — are swept a - way as I'm blessed with priest-hood — pow'r.
in - spi-ra - tion flows lib - er - 'lly when I lis - ten to the — Lord.
strive to live my life faith - ful - ly, I am blessed through priest-hood — pow'r.

Doctrine and Covenants 107:67
Doctrine and Covenants 42:48

166

Priesthood Power

Priesthood Hymns

Nathan Howe

Nathan Howe

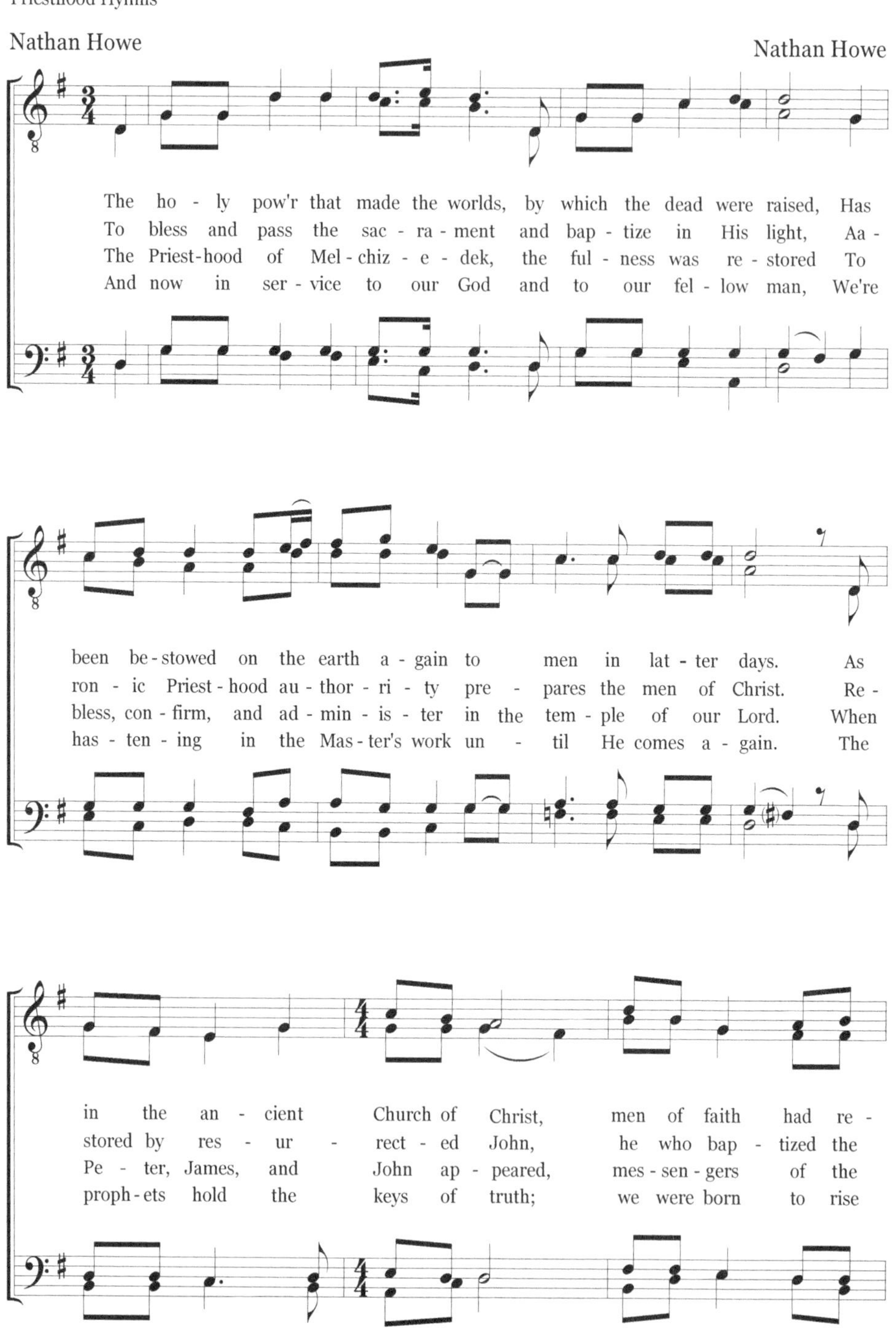
The ho - ly pow'r that made the worlds, by which the dead were raised, Has
To bless and pass the sac - ra - ment and bap - tize in His light, Aa -
The Priest-hood of Mel - chiz - e - dek, the ful - ness was re - stored To
And now in ser - vice to our God and to our fel - low man, We're
been be - stowed on the earth a - gain to men in lat - ter days. As
ron - ic Priest - hood au - thor - ri - ty pre - pares the men of Christ. Re -
bless, con - firm, and ad - min - is - ter in the tem - ple of our Lord. When
has - ten - ing in the Mas - ter's work un - til He comes a - gain. The
in the an - cient Church of Christ, men of faith had re -
stored by res - ur - rect - ed John, he who bap - tized the
Pe - ter, James, and John ap - peared, mes - sen - gers of the
proph - ets hold the keys of truth; we were born to rise

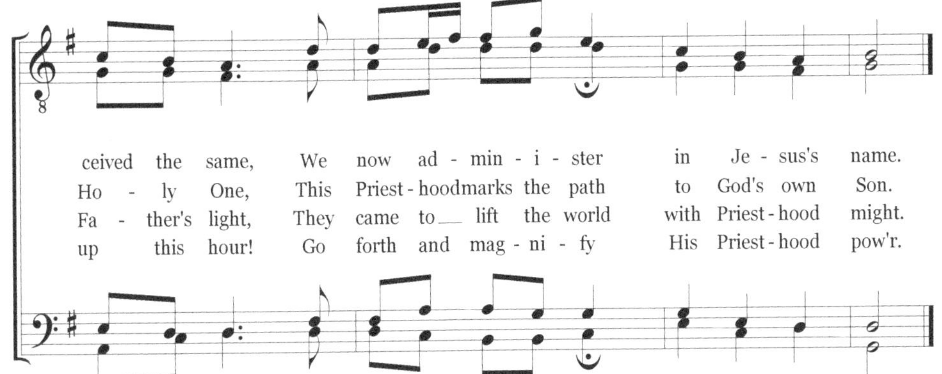
ceived the same, We now ad - min - i - ster in Je - sus's name.
Ho - ly One, This Priest - hood marks the path to God's own Son.
Fa - ther's light, They came to lift the world with Priest - hood might.
up this hour! Go forth and mag - ni - fy His Priest - hood pow'r.

1 Peter 2:5
1 Peter 2:9

167 Steadfast and Immovable

Relief Society Hymns

Annette W. Dickman

Annette W. Dickman

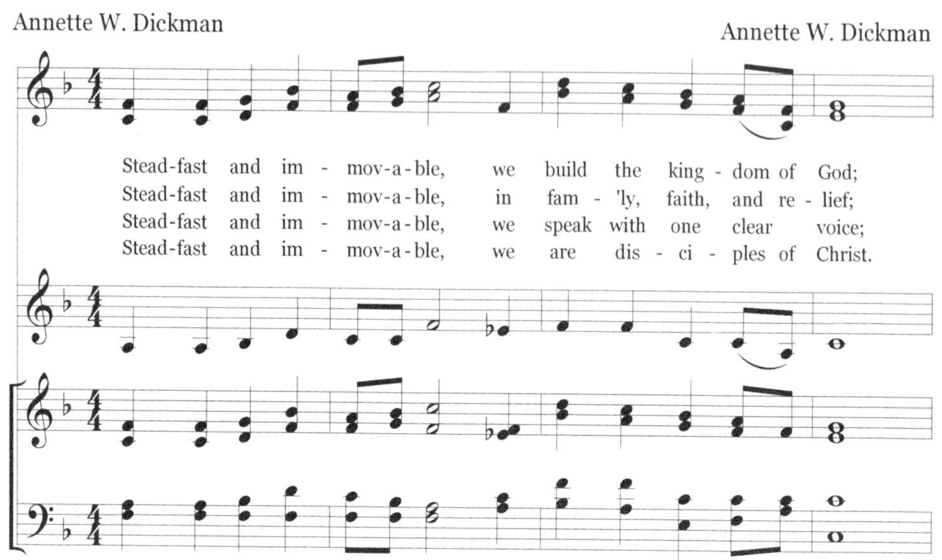

Stead-fast and im - mov-a-ble, we build the king - dom of God;
Stead-fast and im - mov-a-ble, in fam - 'ly, faith, and re - lief;
Stead-fast and im - mov-a-ble, we speak with one clear voice;
Stead-fast and im - mov-a-ble, we are dis - ci - ples of Christ.

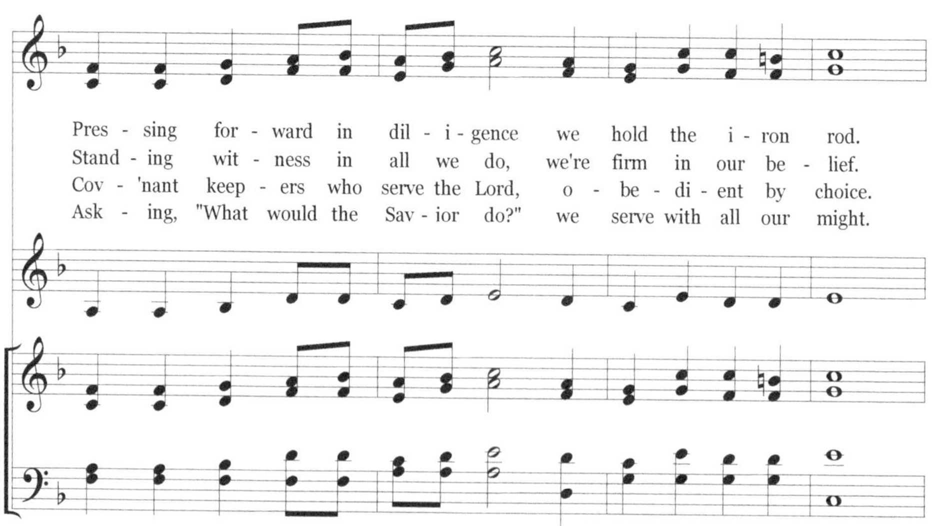

Pres - sing for - ward in dil - i - gence we hold the i - ron rod.
Stand - ing wit - ness in all we do, we're firm in our be - lief.
Cov - 'nant keep - ers who serve the Lord, o - be - di - ent by choice.
Ask - ing, "What would the Sav - ior do?" we serve with all our might.

Dai - ly we pray to know God's will and strive to o - bey, His
Teach - ing our val - ues in all we say, we strength - en our homes in
Lis - ten - ing to our proph - et's call, we fol - low his coun - sel
Bles - sing the ones who stand in need, the law of the gos - pel

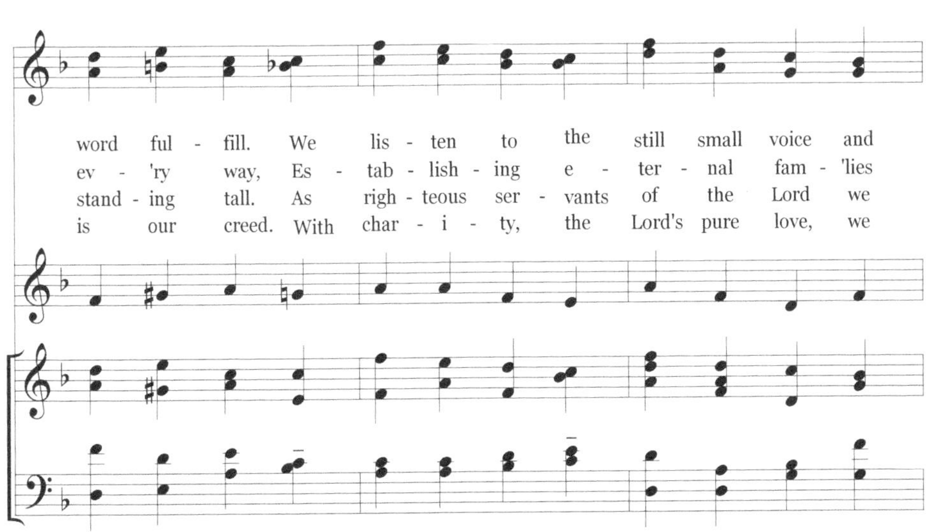
word ful - fill. We lis - ten to the still small voice and
ev - 'ry way, Es - tab - lish - ing e - ter - nal fam - 'lies
stand - ing tall. As righ - teous ser - vants of the Lord we
is our creed. With char - i - ty, the Lord's pure love, we

fol - low its guid - ing word.
sealed in joy com - plete.
grate - ful - ly re - joice.
live and share His light.

Mosiah 5:15

168 The Priesthood Is Restored

Priesthood Hymns

Joan D. Campbell, Verse 2 William P. Merill

Hal K. Campbell, arr. Esther Megargel

The

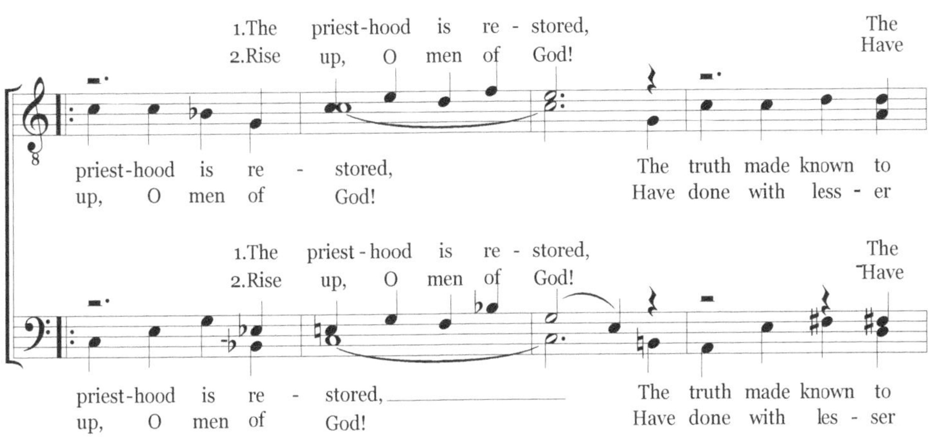
1.The priest-hood is re - stored,
2.Rise up, O men of God!
The
Have
priest-hood is re - stored,
up, O men of God!
The truth made known to
Have done with less - er
1.The priest - hood is re - stored,
2.Rise up, O men of God!
The
Have
priest-hood is re - stored,
up, O men of God!
The truth made known to
Have done with les - ser

truth made known to man,
done with less - er things.
man,
things.
That God has spo - ken to the earth, His
Give heart and soul and mind and strength To
truth made known - to man,
done with les ser things.
man,
things.

pow'r is here a - gain.
serve the King of
2.Rise kings. To serve the King of kings.

2 Nephi 1:23
Moroni 10:31

169

The Priesthood Keys

Priesthood Hymns

Gary Croxall
Kathleen Holyoak
In lat - ter days the Lord re - stored the priest - hood keys to men.
No man can take the priest-hood pow'r up - on him - self to bear,
Each or - di - nance the Lord re - quires de - mands the priest - hood seal,
God's pow - er is a - vail - a - ble up - on the earth a - gain. The
un - less he's called as Aa - ron was by proph - e - cy and prayer. The
and by its sanc - tion and its pow'r each cov - e - nant is real. With -
pow'r to act in God's own name, per - form - ing all His rites, en -
lay - ing on of hands con - fers God's priest - hood on a man. But
out the priest - hood and its rites, the pow'r of god - li - ness is
a - bles man to be im - bued with spir - it and with light.
one must have au - thor - i - ty to preach and lay on hands.
not re - vealed to men on earth and is not man - i - fest.

Doctrine and Covenants 84:19
Doctrine and Covenants 128:11

170

A Part of You

Benedictions

Linda Pratt
Linda Pratt
We're sad to see you go a-way, but part of you will al-ways stay. Here
deep in-side will be a place to keep your hap-py smil-ing face. Re-mem-ber hap-py
voic-es, when we are far a-part. And take our smil-ing fac-es and lock them in your
heart. So, though we're sad to see you go, Down deep in-side, we'll al-ways know. We'll
keep you here, you'll keep us too. We'll al-ways have a part of you.

2 Corinthians 13:11

171

Benedictions

God, Be Thou with Me

Saturn Primer adapted

Jason Robison

God, be Thou in my head. Raise Thou my un-der - stand-ing.
God, be Thou with mine eyes, Guide me in my seek - ing.
Be Thou in my mouth and in my speak - ing. God, be
in my, in my think - ing. God, be Thou at mine

end, And at my de - part - ing.
Music © 2015 Jason Robison
John 14:16
John 14:23

172 God Be with You Till We Meet Again

Benedictions

Jeremiah E. Rankin
William B. Bradbury, arr. Brent Yorgason
God be with you till we meet a - gain; By His coun - sels guide, up - hold you; With His sheep se - cure - ly fold you. God be with you till we meet a - gain.
God be with you till we meet a - gain; When life's per - ils thick con - found you, Put His arms un - fail - ing round you. God be with you till we meet a - gain.
God be with you till we meet a - gain; Keep love's ban - ner float - ing o'er you; Smite death's threat - 'ning wave be - fore you. God be with you till we meet a - gain.

2 Thessalonians 3:16
Numbers 6:24-26

173 God Welcomes His Servants Back Home

Benedictions

Kevin G. Pace
Michael D. Young
Shed - ding their shack - les of mor - tal life, God
Tak - ing the bur - dens of their mor - tal load, God
Greet - ing with joy, all those whom they love, God
wel - comes His ser - vants back home. Prom - is - ing rest from their
wel - comes His ser - vants back home. Of - fer - ing peace from the
wel - comes His ser - vants back home. Seat - ing them down in
mor - tal strife, God wel - comes His ser - vants back home. How
per - il - ous road, God wel - comes His ser - vants back home. How
man - sions a - bove, God wel - comes His ser - vants back home. How
pre - cious the life in ser - vice giv'n! How pre - cious the glimpse of
wor - thy the life that res - cues the lost! How wor - thy the one who asks
glo - rious the life lived true to the end. How glo - rious the gift through them

earth - ly heav'n! Shed - ing their shack - les of mor - tal life, God
not the cost! Tak - ing the bur - dens of their mor - tal load, God
God did send. Greet - ing with joy, with all whom they love, God
wel - comes His ser - vants back home.
wel - comes His ser - vants back home.
wel - comes His ser - vants back home.

Matthew 25:21-23

174 Old Irish Blessing

Benedictions

Traditional Irish Blessing

Arr. Michael D. Young

May the road now rise to meet you. May the wind be at your back,___ The
May the grace of God go with you. May His an - gels go be - fore___ you.
May our love go al - so with you. May it warm you through our part___ ting.
sun shine warm up - on your face,___ The rain fall soft - ly up - on your fields. Till we
May His Spir - it's voice im - plore___ you. May the grace of God go with you.
Greet the glo - rious day that's start - ing. May our love go al - so with you.
meet,_______ Till we meet,___ May God hold you in___ His___
hand. Till we meet,___ Till we meet, May God hold you in His hand.

John 14:27

175
Benedictions

The Lord Bless You and Keep You

Traditional Text

Michael D. Young

The Lord bless you and keep you. The Lord make His face to shine up-on
you, And be gra - cious un - to you, And be gra - cious un - to you. The
Lord lift up the light of His coun-te-nance up - on you, up - on you, and
give you peace, and give you peace.

Numbers 6:24
Alma 7:25

176 When Shall We All Meet Again?

Benedictions

Parley P. Pratt

Jason Robison

When shall we all meet a - gain? When shall we our
We to for - eign climes re - pair; Truth, the mes - sage
Now the bright and morn - ing star Spreads its glo - rious
When the sons of Is - rael come, When they build Je -
When the earth is cleansed by fire; When the wick - ed's

rest ob - tain? When our pil - grim - age be o'er
which we bear; Truth, which an - gels oft have borne;
light a - far, Kin - dles up the ris - ing dawn
ru - sa - lem; When the house of God is reared,
hopes ex - pire, When in cold o - bliv - ion's shade,

Part - ing sighs be known no more; When Mount Zi - on
Truth to com - fort those who mourn. Truth e - ter - nal
Of that bright mil - len - nial morn; When the Saints shall
And Mes - si - ah's way pre - pared; When from Heav'n He
Proud op - pres - sors all are laid; Long will Zi - on's

we re - gain, There may we all meet a - gain.
will re - main, On its rock we'll meet a - gain.
rise and reign, Then may we all meet a - gain.
comes to reign, In the clouds we'll meet a - gain.
Mount re - main, There we all may meet a - gain.

Alma 17:13
Moroni 10:34

About the Author

Though Michael grew up traveling the world with his military father, he now lives in Utah with his wife, Jen, and his two sons. He played for several years with the handbell choir Bells on Temple Square and is now a member of the Tabernacle Choir at Temple Square. He is the author of the novels in The Canticle Kingdom series, The Last Archangel series, the Chess Quest series and the *Penultimate Dawn Cycle* (*The Hunger*), as well as the nonfiction work, *The Song of the Righteous*.

Musical Notes

Musical Notes

Musical Notes

Musical Notes

Musical Notes